embroidery
basics

embroidery
basics

all you need to know to start stitching

Betty Barnden

BARRON'S

A QUARTO BOOK

Copyright © 2005 by Quarto Inc.

First edition for North America published in 2005 by Barron's Educational Series, Inc.

All inquiries should be addressed to:
Barron's Educational Series, Inc.
250 Wireless Boulevard
Hauppauge, New York 11788
www.barronseduc.com

ISBN-13: 978-0-7641-5822-3
ISBN-10: 0-7641-5822-8

Library of Congress Catalog Card No. 2004107402

QUAR.EBA

Conceived, designed, and produced by
Quarto Publishing plc
The Old Brewery
6 Blundell Street
London
N7 9BH

Project Editor Susie May
Art Editor Anna Knight
*Assistant Art Directo*r Penny Cobb
Designer Penny Dawes
Illustrator Kate Simunek
Photographers Colin Bowling, Martin Norris,
    Paul Forrester
Copy Editor Claire Waite Brown
Proofreader Robert Harries
Indexer Pamela Ellis

Art Director Moira Clinch
Publisher Paul Carslake

Color separation by ProVision Pte Ltd, Singapore
Printed and bound by Star Standard Industries (Pte) Ltd, Singapore

9 8 7 6 5 4 3 2 1

CONTENTS

Introduction	6
Tools and Materials	8
Basic Techniques	14

COUNTED THREAD EMBROIDERY 24

Cross-stitch guidelines	26
PROJECT 1 – **Greeting card**	28
Counted stitches on Aida fabric	30
Evenweave guidelines	32
Assisi work	33
PROJECT 2 – **Scented sachets**	34
Blackwork	36
PROJECT 3 – **Pot holder**	38
Half cross-stitch on canvas	40
PROJECT 4 – **Book cover**	41
Canvaswork guidelines	42
PROJECT 5 – **Photo frame**	44
Using waste canvas	46
PROJECT 6 – **Heart napkin**	47
Hardanger work	48
PROJECT 7 – **Trinket box**	50

Beads and sequins	52	
Special threads	53	
PROJECT 8 – **Sparkly beaded purse**	54	

FREESTYLE EMBROIDERY 56

Tracing designs	58
Freestyle embroidery guidelines	59
PROJECT 9 – **Rabbit cushion**	60
Transferring designs	62
Photo-transfers	64
PROJECT 10 – **Framed portrait**	66
Choosing and using stabilizers	68
PROJECT 11 – **Flowery T-shirt**	72
Simple appliqué	74
PROJECT 12 – **Chef's apron**	76

STITCH LIBRARY 76

Backstitch	80
Double running stitch	82
Running stitch	84
Half cross-stitch	85
Cross-stitch	86

Part cross-stitches	88
Upright cross-stitch	90
Star stitch	91
Fan and ray stitches	92
Algerian eye stitch	94
Hardanger stitches	96
Herringbone stitch	104
Blanket stitch	106
Chain and single chain stitches	108
Satin stitch	110
Stem stitch	113
Fly stitch	114
Seeding stitch	115
French knots	116
Bullion knots	118
Feather stitch	120
Simple couching	122

Glossary	124
Resources	125
Index	126
Credits	128

INTRODUCTION

Embroidery is the art of decorating fabric with needle and thread. This book will introduce you to a wide range of embroidery techniques, from simple stylized cross-stitch to the more flowing, natural forms you can achieve in freestyle embroidery.

Many different techniques and styles have developed over the centuries in different parts of the world. These divide into two main groups: counted thread embroidery and freestyle embroidery. Counted thread embroidery includes techniques such as cross-stitch, blackwork, Hardanger work, and canvaswork; the stitches are normally counted from a chart, working on an evenly woven fabric or canvas. Freestyle embroidery takes no account of the fabric weave, and the stitches flow freely, following a design drawn on the fabric surface.

The **Materials and Equipment** chapter shows all the items you need to get started, plus other accessories you may want to acquire as you progress. The right choice of thread, fabric, and needles will help you succeed with any project.

Basic Techniques are explained with step-by-step photographs. From threading your needle to stretching fabric in a hoop, these techniques are common to many types of embroidery.

In the **Counted Thread** and **Freestyle** sections, the working method for each type of embroidery is described in detail, again with step-by-step photographs. Once you have learned each basic method, try making the project that follows. The techniques and projects progress from cross-stitch through the associated counted thread techniques, then from simple freestyle outline designs through techniques for embroidery on various fabrics, ending with appliqué work. You can work through these sections in order, trying out the various methods to find out which you enjoy most, or jump in at any point to learn a particular type of embroidery that interests you.

The **Stitch Library** includes all the stitches used for the projects in the book, and a few more. The method of forming each stitch is explained and illustrated with step-by-step photographs. Embroidered samples reproduced full-size show the various uses of each stitch.

This book contains all the information you need to explore the intriguing art of embroidery. Modern materials, equipment, and products enable us to create our own versions of traditional designs with an up-to-date twist, and inspire us to experiment to find our own language of stitches. Enjoy the colors and textures of fabrics and threads, the simplicity of a cross-stitch design, or the sinuous curves of freestyle embroidery. Give pleasure to others by creating beautiful gifts and keepsakes for your family and friends. Welcome to your new hobby!

THREADS

There are many different types of embroidery thread, in a wide range of fibers and colors. Some threads can be used for several types of embroidery; others are designed for a particular purpose. Get to know the different threads that are available, and start collecting now.

COTTON THREADS

Soft embroidery cotton
A heavyweight, lightly twisted matte thread with a soft, muted appearance, suitable for stitching on canvas and coarse fabrics.

Cotton embroidery floss (stranded cotton)
A skein is usually formed of six fine strands loosely wound together. You can use any number of strands for stitching, making this a very versatile thread. Cotton floss is available in hundreds of plain colors, as well as shaded and random-dyed effects. This is the most popular thread, useful for many types of embroidery from cross-stitch to freestyle.

Perle cotton
Perle cotton is a firm, twisted thread with a glossy finish, sold in skeins or on spools. Perle cotton No. 3 is the heaviest and No. 5 (medium-weight) the most common. Nos. 8 (fine) and 12 (very fine) are also available. This thread may not be divided into strands. It makes firm, bold stitches with a clear outline.

CORDS AND BRAIDS
These are mainly used for couching or as trims, rather than for embroidery stitches. Cords are round while braids are flat, like a ribbon, but loosely woven for flexibility.

WOOLS

Tapestry wool

This pure wool yarn is similar in weight to double knitting yarn. It is sold in small skeins and a huge range of colors. Use it for stitching on canvas.

Persian wool

Skeins consist of three strands loosely wound together. Any number of strands may be combined, making this a versatile yarn suitable for any gauge of canvas.

SILKY THREADS

Silk floss

Like cotton floss, this thread may be stranded (four or six strands) in a skein, or on a spool. The soft sheen of silk adds a touch of luxury to any embroidery on fabric.

Viscose rayon floss

This floss is an imitation silk thread, sold as a stranded skein or on a spool. It is sometimes tricky to handle, but has a beautiful sheen and depth of color.

BEADS AND SEQUINS

Beads and sequins can be used together with threads to add an extra sparkle to your embroidery.

Beads

A huge variety of beads is available, from tiny seed beads—often used to enhance cross-stitch projects—through to chunky glass, wood, or plastic beads used to trim tassels or ties. Shapes include globes, doughnuts, and tubes—called bugle beads. Whatever your project, there's a bead to suit.

Sequins

Sequins are flat shapes, sometimes crinkled or stamped, cut from metallic foil, with a hole for stitching them onto fabric. As well as the usual round sequins in various sizes, you will find stars, leaves, snowflakes, and other fancy shapes in a wide range of colors.

METALLIC THREADS

Blending filament

Very fine metallic blending filament may be used alone, or combined with other threads to add a subtle shine to any color.

Synthetic metallic threads

Sometimes called Lurex threads, these were originally developed to imitate true metal threads of real gold and silver. They are available today not just in gold and silver, but in a wide variety of colors and weights, so a suitable substitute may be found for any weight of thread.

FABRICS

The various fabrics used for embroidery suit particular methods of stitching, so Aida and evenweave fabrics are used for counted thread embroidery such as cross-stitch, canvas is used for canvaswork, and plain fabrics for freestyle embroidery.

6-count white

AIDA FABRIC

Aida fabric is evenly woven—usually from cotton—with a specific number of squares to the inch (2.5 cm), called the "count." The weave forms a pattern of little squares and tiny holes, making it easy to form regular stitches. Counts range from 6-count (often called Binca fabric) suitable for beginners' projects, through 8-count, 10-count, 11-count, 12-count, 14-count (the most popular size for cross-stitch) to 18-count, the finest size usually used for cross-stitch. The popular sizes are available in a wide range of colors.

28-count lilac slubby linen | 32-count cream linen

28-count pink cotton

△ EVENWEAVE FABRIC

Evenweave fabrics are woven with a specific number of threads—rather than squares—to the inch (2.5 cm), again called the "count." Counts range from 18-count (coarse) through to 36-count (very fine). They are available in cotton, linen, and various blended fibers, and a wide range of colors. They may be used for all types of counted thread embroidery, and finer counts may also be used for freestyle embroidery.

11-count white

▽ HARDANGER FABRIC

This is similar to Aida fabric, but 20-, 22-, or 24-count are the usual sizes for Hardanger work. The fabric is often treated with a softening finish that makes it easier to cut and withdraw the threads for Hardanger work. White, cream, and a range of soft colors are available.

14-count blue

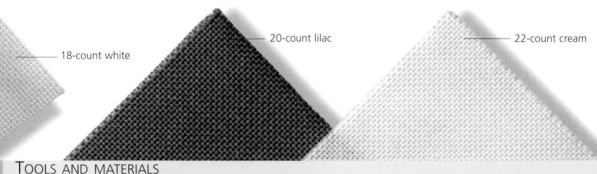

20-count lilac

22-count cream

18-count white

18-gauge white   14-gauge natural

12-gauge white

Canvas

△ Cotton or linen canvas

Canvas is also woven with a specific number of threads—or sometimes pairs of threads—to the inch (2.5 cm). The "gauge" or "mesh count" of canvas is the number of holes per inch (2.5 cm). Common gauges for embroidery range from 8-gauge (coarse) through 10-gauge, 12-gauge, and 14-gauge—popular for stitching with wool—to 18-gauge or finer still. Canvas is normally woven from strong cotton or linen, either white or natural, and stitching usually covers the canvas completely.

▷ Plastic canvas

Plastic canvas is molded in sheets. Various gauges and colors are available. Heavier types may be used to construct boxes and other three-dimensional forms.

14-gauge ivory

▽ Plain fabrics

Plain weave fabrics are normally used for freestyle embroidery, when the design is stitched without reference to the woven surface. The beginner should choose fairly smooth, non-stretch, woven fabrics in natural fibers such as cotton, linen, or silk, along with a suitable weight of thread and size of needle (see page 59). Fabrics containing synthetic fibers can be difficult to embroider. Lightweight and stretch fabrics, such as cotton jersey, require backing with stabilizer (see page 68).

10-gauge clear

▽ Waste canvas

Waste canvas is a special type of canvas, loosely woven but stiffened with a water-soluble glue so that when wet, the threads may be easily pulled apart. It is used to stitch counted thread designs onto plain fabric. It is normally only available in 14-count and has a distinctive blue stripe woven in, so it cannot be mistaken for ordinary canvas.

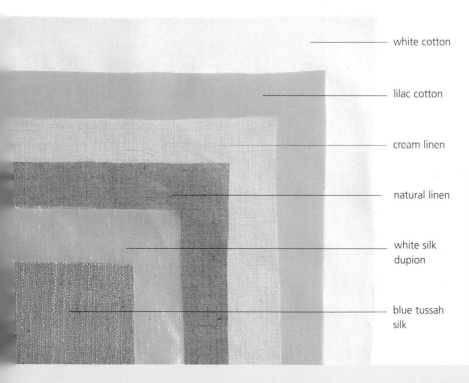

white cotton

lilac cotton

cream linen

natural linen

white silk dupion

blue tussah silk

14-count waste canvas

EQUIPMENT

Choose the right needle to suit your fabric and thread. Good quality needles are the stitcher's most important tool. Cheap needles are sometimes rough around the eyes, so threads fray quickly; they often break easily; and they don't glide through the fabric as they should. Buy specialist embroidery needles and choose the right size to suit your thread (see the tables on pages 26, 40, 48 and 59). With each type of needle, the higher the size number, the finer the needle. There are a few other items you will find you need to collect. In general, embroidery equipment is not expensive, and you can purchase these extras as you need them.

NEEDLES

Tapestry needles

Choose blunt-tip tapestry needles for counted thread embroidery on Aida and evenweave fabrics, and for canvaswork. The blunt tip helps you stitch neatly through the fabric or canvas holes without splitting fabric threads. Tapestry needles have a long, slim eyes that are easy to thread. Choose tapestry needles in sizes 13 (large) through to 26 or 28 (very fine).

Sharp needles

For freestyle embroidery on plain fabrics or on evenweave, choose needles with sharp points. Embroidery or crewel needles are fine, sharp needles sized from 1 to 10, with an elongated eye to hold two or more strands of floss. Chenille needles are similar to tapestry needles, but with a sharp point, sized from 13 to 26.

OTHER EQUIPMENT

Tweezers

Pointed tweezers are used when unpicking stitches, and also for withdrawing threads for Hardanger work. A pair with an attached magnifier is useful for both operations.

Pins

For assembling projects, you will need dressmakers' steel pins. For blocking canvaswork, pins with large heads, T-pins, or push pins are useful.

Scissors

For cutting threads neatly you need small, sharp scissors, and for Hardanger work they should be as finely pointed as possible. For cutting fabric use dressmakers' shears. For cutting paper use an old pair.

Ruler and tape measure

Use a ruler for checking the count of Aida or evenweave fabric. A tape measure is useful when marking and finishing large projects. Buy a new tape measure because the first few inches tend to stretch after a while.

Fabric markers

These are used to mark fabric temporarily. Special pens may be water-soluble—misting or rinsing with water removes the marks—or vanishing—the marks vanish after about 48 hours. A quilters' or dressmakers' chalk pencil is useful for marking dark fabrics, and the marks may be brushed or washed away.

Blocking board

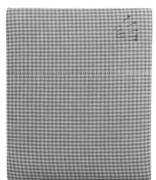

This is used for blocking finished embroidery, especially canvaswork. Make your own by covering a piece of board about 12- or 18-in. (30- or 45-cm) square with a layer of batting, then a layer of fabric stretched tightly and glued or stapled to the back of the board. Gingham fabric provides a useful guide to blocking your work square.

Embroidery frames

These interlocking bars are available in pairs in a range of lengths, so you can choose two pairs to fit any size of embroidery. The fabric is fixed to the frame with staples or thumbtacks, so the system is only suitable for fairly heavy fabrics, but ideal for canvaswork.

Slate frames are available in several sizes. The fabric is basted to the webbing fixed to the top and bottom rollers, the rollers tightened, and the fabric edges laced to the sides of the frame. The fabric width must fit inside the frame width, but the fabric can be any length, with the excess length wound onto the rollers.

Embroidery hoops

An embroidery hoop consists of two rings, one fitting inside the other. The screw adjustment allows you to suit the fit to any thickness of fabric. If possible, choose a size that will hold the complete design, so the hoop will not need repositioning as work progresses.

FOR ASSEMBLING PROJECTS

Sewing machine

A basic sewing machine will speed up the assembly of most projects, but if you don't have one, you can sew by hand.

Hand sewing

For sewing seams and hems use ordinary hand sewing needles. Choose a pack of mixed sizes so you can suit the needle to the fabric.

Thread

You will also need ordinary sewing thread. Choose a color to match your fabric. For cottons and linens choose cotton thread; polyester thread is really only suited to polyester fabric. Silk thread is best for silk fabrics.

Thimble

A thimble is not always necessary, but useful at times. Choose one that fits your middle (second) finger comfortably.

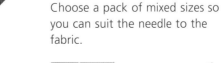

BASIC TECHNIQUES

These general techniques are common to many of the projects in this book,

and you'll find them useful for other projects of your own.

CUTTING FABRIC AND CANVAS

STEP 1 Any fabric or canvas is normally cut "straight with the grain," that is, along the straight lines of the woven threads (unless, of course, you are cutting a curved shape). Use dressmakers' shears, or large, sharp scissors. If you are using a hoop, cut a square of fabric at least 1 in. (2.5 cm) larger all around than the hoop. Or cut the size given in project instructions.

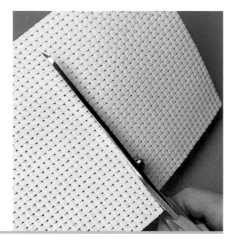

STEP 2 To avoid frayed edges, overcast with ordinary sewing thread or machine stitch with a wide zigzag. For canvas see page 40.

BASTING CENTER LINES FOR COUNTED THREAD WORK

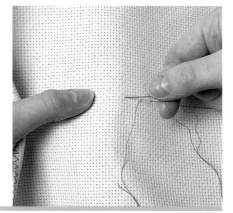

STEP 1 For designs counted from charts, you need to mark the center lines with basting. Fold the fabric in half and press lightly with your fingers to mark the fold line. Open the fabric out flat and use a tapestry needle and sewing thread to baste along the fold line, following a straight line of holes.

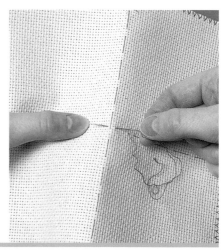

STEP 2 Fold the fabric in half in the other direction and baste the second center line in the same way. Where the two lines of basting cross marks the center of the fabric.

MOUNTING IN A HOOP

Use a hoop for Aida, evenweave, or plain fabric, but not for canvas.

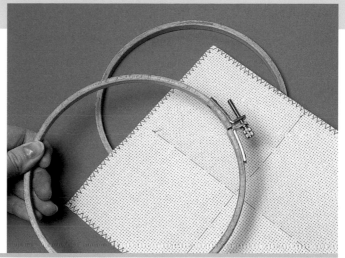

STEP 1
If necessary, iron the fabric flat and square. Adjust the size of the outer ring of the hoop, by means of the screw, so that it fits quite snugly over the inner ring. Lay the inner ring on a flat surface with the fabric centered on top.

STEP 2
Push the outer ring gently into place. It should fit firmly, holding the fabric flat and taut. If it won't fit, loosen the screw slightly. Never adjust the screw with the fabric in place, or you may damage the fabric, so always remove the fabric if you need to adjust the screw.

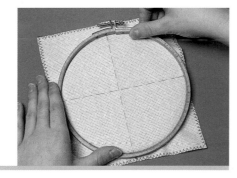

STEP 3
To release the fabric, push the inner ring away with your thumbs. Never leave your work mounted in the hoop when you are not working on it, because the hoop may leave a permanent mark.

PLASTIC HOOP FRAME

This type of plastic hoop frame has a flexible outer ring that simply pushes into place. You can work the embroidery, trim away the excess fabric at the back, and hang it on the wall.

TIPS
• If the fabric is too small for the hoop, baste strips of waste fabric to the edges.
• To protect delicate fabric, mount it together with a layer of tissue paper on each side, then tear away the tissue over and under the stitching area.

MOUNTING IN A SLATE FRAME
Use a slate frame for any type of fabric or canvas.

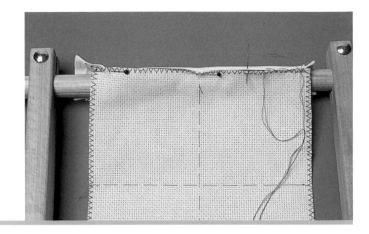

STEP 1 The fabric should be narrower than the
frame in one direction. In the other direction, fabric of any
length may be wound onto the rollers. Mark the center of
the webbing on each roller, and match the center of the
fabric to this. Pin the edge of the fabric to the webbing and
use ordinary sewing thread and a sharp needle to overcast
the fabric edge to the webbing. Do this on both rollers.

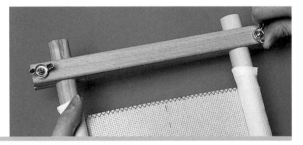

STEP 2 Wind the fabric
onto the rollers so the area to be
embroidered is stretched between
the rollers, then tighten the roller
wing nuts.

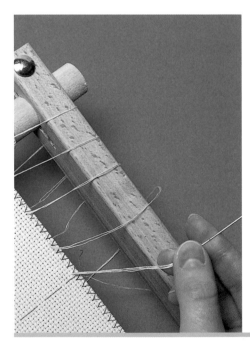

STEP 3 With large embroideries it is a good idea to lace
the side edges to the side bars with strong thread—the fabric
edges may be temporarily reinforced by sewing on lengths of
cotton tape if necessary. If the embroidery is longer than the
frame, embroider one end completely, undo the lacing,
reposition the fabric by adjusting the rollers, then lace the side
edges again in the new position to finish the embroidery.

INTERLOCKING BAR FRAMES

Use this type of frame for small projects on stout fabric or canvas, but not for
lightweight fabrics. Choose two pairs of bars to suit the
canvas size. Push them together to make the frame,
then use thumbtacks or staples to hold the
canvas or fabric in place.

▽ HANDLING SKEINS OF FLOSS (STRANDED THREAD)

Cotton, silk, and rayon threads are often supplied in skeins with several strands wound loosely together. If you pull out the end that comes from the middle of the skein, the skein will stay together and not lose its label. You may need only one, two, or three strands for your stitching. Cut an 18-in. (46-cm) length of thread, then separate the strands at one end and pull them out gently, one by one. Re-combine as many strands as you need, then thread your needle.

△ HANDLING SKEINS OF PERLE COTTON

Larger skeins of perle cotton are twisted to keep them neat. Untwist the skein and snip the knot where the ends are tied together. If you cut right across the skein at this point, you will have lots of lengths of thread ready for stitching. To keep unused lengths tidy in your workbox, double them and tie a loose overhand knot.

THREADING NEEDLES

Use this method for any standard thread or floss.

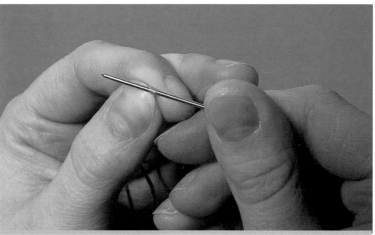

STEP 1 Fold one end of the thread over the needle tip and hold it tightly.

STEP 2 Slip the needle out, leaving a tiny loop. Push the needle eye down over the loop. Pull the loop through until the short tail is free.

TIPS
- As a rule, never stitch with more than 18 in. (46 cm) of thread.
- Some threads have a smooth and a rough direction: Run a length between your fingertips, or across your lips, to feel the difference. Thread the smooth end first through the needle.
- To thread bulky or very fine threads, see page 53.

To thread bulky or very fine threads, see page 53.

STARTING THREADS

There are three ways of starting new threads, depending on the stitch and design you are working.

Stitch-to-the-knot method

Use this method for cross-stitch, half cross-stitch, and any other stitch that will enclose the thread end on the wrong side.

STEP 1
Make a small knot at the end of the thread and pass the needle down through the fabric about 1 in. (2.5 cm) away from where your first stitch will be, along the line of the first few stitches. Bring the needle up again where required and pull through so the knot lies on the surface.

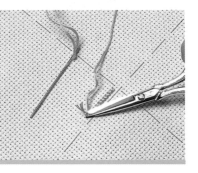

STEP 2
Embroider the first line of stitches up to the knot. On the wrong side, the stitches should enclose the thread leading to the knot. Snip off the knot and continue stitching.

Waste-knot method

Use this method for any type of stitching.

Make a small knot at the end of the thread. Take the needle down through the fabric about 3 in. (7.5 cm) away from where the first stitch will be. Bring the needle up where the embroidery begins and pull it through so the knot lies on the surface. Work the stitches you require, without catching or covering the thread lying across the wrong side. At the end of the stitching, fasten off the thread as below. Then snip off the knot at the beginning, thread this tail into the needle, and fasten it off in the same way.

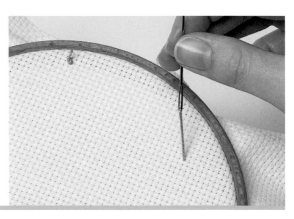

Slip-through-the-back method

Once you have worked the first stitches, you can use this method to begin a new color or thread, provided the new stitches are right up against the old ones.

Slip the needle through the backs of previous stitches for about 1 in. (2.5 cm). Pull through so only the end of the thread is enclosed. Bring the needle through to the right side where required and hold the enclosed thread end firmly in place with your finger and thumb while you work the first couple of stitches.

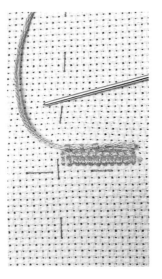

FASTENING OFF A THREAD

When you want to fasten off a thread, either because you've finished with that color or you've used up the length and need another, end with the needle on the wrong side of the work. Slip the needle through the backs of stitches of the same color for about 1 in. (2.5 cm), pull through, and snip off the thread tail.

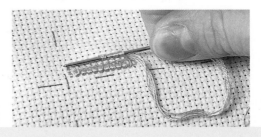

STITCHING METHODS: STAB OR SEW?

Most stitches can be formed in two ways: by stabbing or by sewing. Sometimes one method works best, sometimes the other, and sometimes it's a matter of which you prefer.

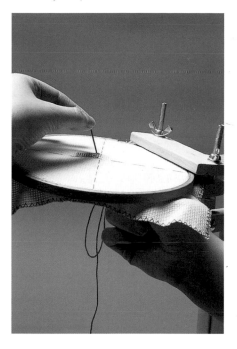

Stab method

As a rule, use this method when working in a hoop or frame. It may seem slow, but your stitches will be neat and accurate. The down and up movements are made separately, keeping the needle at right angles to the surface of the fabric.

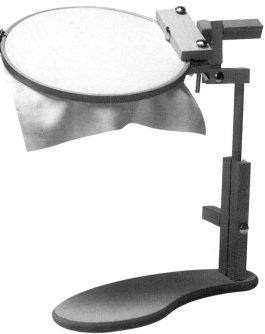

Push the needle partway into the fabric where required, let go, then pull it through from below, tightening the thread (first movement). Slide the needle tip across the underneath of the fabric to find the right place to bring it up again, then push it partway through from below. Let go, then pull the needle through from the top (second movement). With practice, you can use one hand under the work and the other on top.

A hoop or frame stand is useful to keep both hands free.

Sew method

You can use this method when working without a hoop or frame. Some freestyle stitches can be worked this way even when the fabric is in a hoop. Use this method to obtain fluid lines with stitches such as stem stitch.

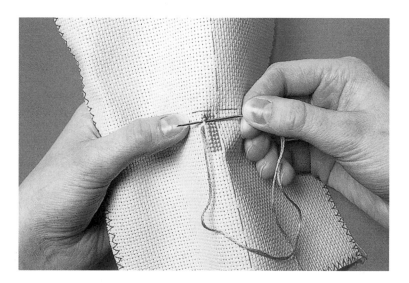

Slide the needle into the fabric, keeping it almost flat with the fabric surface. Manipulate the fabric into position with your free hand (thumb on top, forefinger underneath) so you can push the needle partway out again. Let go of the needle, then pull it through from the sharp end to tighten the thread.

TROUBLESHOOTING

Sometimes you miscount your cross-stitches, or use the wrong color thread, or embroider a couple of stitches that just don't look right. Don't panic; you can fix it.

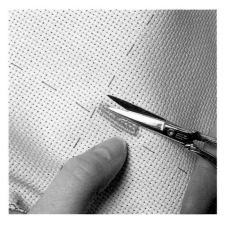

To unpick a couple of stitches

Take the thread out of the needle. Use the needle tip to gently lift out the last stitch you made, then the next, back to the mistake. The thread will probably be frayed, so fasten it off and start again with a fresh thread. Enlarged holes in the fabric will disappear when the embroidery is pressed or blocked.

To unpick several stitches

On the wrong side of the work, use fine, sharp scissors to snip through the backs of the stitches. Unpick the last few with the needle, as left, so you have a tail to fasten off. Use tweezers to pull out all the scraps of thread.

PRESSING AND BLOCKING

When you have finished your embroidery, it will need pressing or blocking to make it look neat. As a rule, pressing is sufficient for embroideries on Aida, evenweave, or plain fabric, while canvaswork requires blocking, a slower process. However, if you find you can't press a piece of embroidery square, try blocking it.

Pressing

Lay the work face down on a soft, well-padded surface such as a folded towel, to avoid flattening the stitches. Heat the iron to a temperature suitable for your fabric and threads. Press gently, lifting and replacing the iron rather than rubbing it across the work. For cotton fabrics and threads you can use a damp pressing cloth between the embroidery and the iron.

Blocking

Dampen the work on the wrong side with a sponge or water spray and lukewarm water. Lay it face down on the blocking board (see page 13) and pull it to shape. Pin the center of each side in place as shown, with large-headed pins at right angles to the edges. Insert more pins out to the corners. Use lots of pins to keep the canvas edges straight. Allow to dry completely, which may take a day or two. Sometimes you need to repeat the blocking process two or three times before the work will lie completely flat.

SEWING TIPS

A few simple sewing techniques are required to finish the projects

in this book. Don't spoil your project by skimping on the assembly:

Take as much care as you did with the embroidery.

SEWING SEAMS: BACKSTITCH

Most projects include a seam allowance; this may be as little as ¼ in. (6 mm), or as much as ¾ in. (2 cm). This is the distance between the cut edge of the fabric and the stitched seam line.

STEP 1 Matching the edges of the
fabrics to be joined, pin the pieces together. You can baste along the seam line with ordinary sewing thread if you wish. Use a small sharp needle and sewing thread to match the fabric. Secure the thread end with a couple of tiny backstitches in the seam allowance, then backstitch (see page 80) along the seam line, making a continuous line of stitches each about ⅛ in. (3 mm) long. Fasten off with two backstitches in the same place. Pull out any basting. Alternatively, you can machine stitch with straight stitch, following the seam line. Begin and end each line of stitching with two or three stitches in reverse.

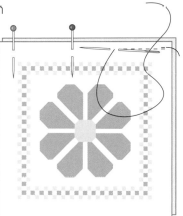

STEP 2 Seams often require
pressing open so that they will lie flat. Open out the seam allowances and use the tip of the iron to press them flat. It is often best to press each seam as it is completed.

STITCHING FROM THE RIGHT SIDE: SLIP STITCH

Slip stitch is almost invisible when worked correctly. Use it to close an opening in a seam (such as after filling an article with stuffing), or to attach a lining inside a purse. It is worked from the right side, with the seam allowances tucked inside between the two layers.

Use a small sharp needle and sewing thread to match the fabric. Secure the thread end to the seam allowance with two tiny backstitches. Insert the needle on the fold line, sliding it between the two layers of the folded edge, and bring it out ⅛ in. (3 mm) farther along the fold. Insert the needle just opposite, inside the fold of the other edge, and bring it out ⅛ in. (3 mm) farther along that fold. Repeat along the seam, drawing the two edges together. Fasten off with two tiny backstitches.

TURNING RIGHT SIDE OUT

When you are making articles such as the scented sachets or sparkly beaded purse (see pages 34 and 54), you need to turn them neatly right side out.

STEP 1 Snip across the seam allowances, close to the stitching, at corners that will be inside the article.

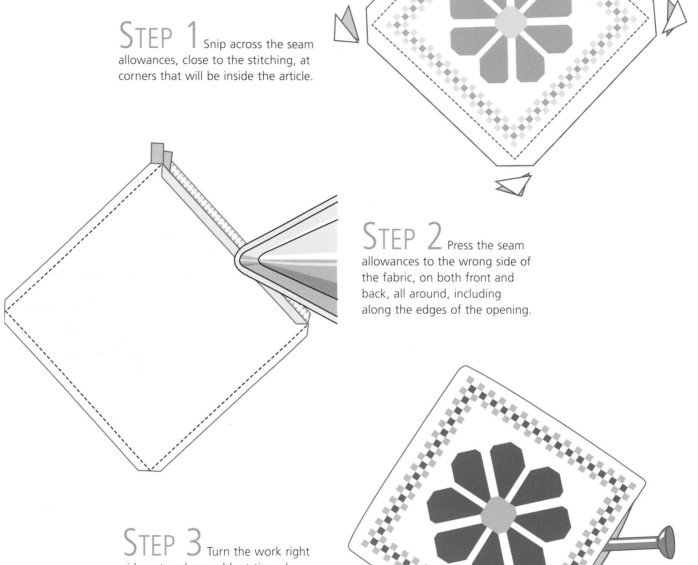

STEP 2 Press the seam allowances to the wrong side of the fabric, on both front and back, all around, including along the edges of the opening.

STEP 3 Turn the work right side out and use a blunt-tipped knitting needle, or something similar, to push out the corners neatly. Press the corners.

TURNING A HEM: HEMSTITCH

A double hem is used to finish a straight edge on a single layer of fabric, such as on the heart napkin (see page 47).

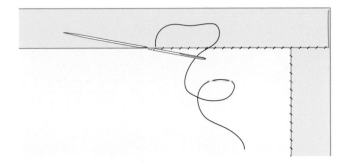

STEP 1 A typical hem allowance is ¾ in. (2 cm). Fold and press ¼ in. (6 mm) to the wrong side of the fabric. Then fold again by ½ in. (14 mm) and press again. Pin the hem in place.

STEP 2 Use a small sharp needle and sewing thread to match the fabric. Secure the thread underneath the first fold with two tiny backstitches. Pick up just two or three fabric threads from the single layer below. Insert the needle just above and slip it through the folded edge, inside the fold, for about ⅛–¼ in. (3–6 mm). Repeat as required. Fasten off with two tiny backstitches on the folded edge. Where two hemmed edges meet at a corner, fold them neatly as shown here. Double hems can also be machine stitched: stitch ⅜ in. (1 cm) from the outside edge, to make sure you catch the first fold in place.

APPLYING BIAS BINDING

Using bias binding is another way to finish a raw fabric edge. The binding is a narrow strip of fabric, cut "on the bias," at 45 degrees to the straight grain, ready-creased with two sharp folds. It may be applied to curved edges that are difficult to hem. It can also be decorative since bias binding may be cotton, satin, or even Lurex fabric and is available in several widths and lots of colors.

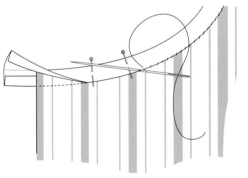

STEP 1 Cut a length of binding about 1 in. (2.5 cm) longer than the edge to be covered. Open it out and match one edge to the edge of the fabric, on the right side. Pin the binding in place, using lots of pins around curves. Use a small sharp needle and sewing thread to match the fabric to backstitch along the fold line nearer to the fabric edge, or machine stitch with straight stitch.

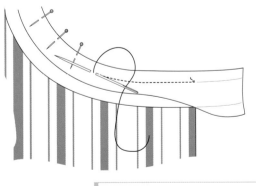

STEP 2 Fold the binding over the raw edge to the wrong side and pin the second fold of the binding to meet the wrong side of the stitched line. Hem stitch (see above) the second fold in place to the back of the first line of stitches. Trim off any excess binding at each end.

TIP
Where an end of the binding will show when the article is finished, open it out completely before Step 1, and press the end to the inside by ¼ in. (6 mm). Apply as above, stitching through both layers at the folded end. Slip stitch the side ends together at the corner for a neat finish.

counted thread
embroidery

In counted thread embroidery, stitches are counted from a chart onto fabric that has a regular weave, such as Aida fabric, evenweave, or canvas. Cross-stitch is the most familiar form of counted thread embroidery, but there are other forms based on the same principles, such as blackwork, Hardanger work, and canvaswork, all explained here.

CROSS-STITCH GUIDELINES

Cross-stitch from a chart is most often worked on Aida fabric. Each colored square or symbol on a chart represents one cross-stitch worked over one woven square of the fabric.

FORMING THE STITCHES

Each cross can be formed exactly as shown below, or the top and bottom diagonal stitches can be worked to slant in the opposite direction. Whichever way you prefer to stitch, remember to be consistent, making sure the top diagonals of each cross slant in the same direction.

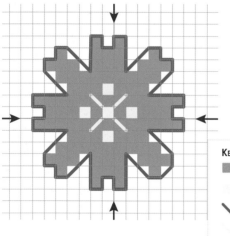

Worked on 11-count Aida fabric, this flower measures about 1¼ in. (3 cm) square. On 14-count fabric it will be 1 in. (2.5 cm) square.

KEY

- ■ Turquoise cross-stitch
- Yellow cross-stitch
- ◣ Blue straight stitches
- Yellow straight stitches

SUITABLE NEEDLES AND THREADS FOR CROSS-STITCH

You can substitute other threads of equivalent thickness to the strands given.

Aida fabric count (holes per inch)	Equivalent evenweave fabric count (threads per inch)	Strands of cotton embroidery floss	Tapestry needle size
6		6	18 or 20
8		5	22
11	22	3	22
14	28	2 or 3	24
16	32	2	24 or 26
18		2	26
22		1	26

STEP 1

Prepare Aida fabric for counted thread work with overcast edges and basted center lines. Mount the fabric in a hoop or frame.

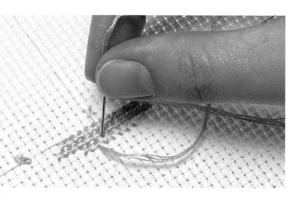

STEP 2
Choose a suitable needle and floss from the table. Identify each color or symbol on the chart with the corresponding shade of floss. Begin at or near the center to avoid miscounting. Begin with the stitch-to-the-knot method. Work the crosses singly, or in lines, depending on the design.

STEP 3
To finish off a thread, run the needle through the backs of the stitches in the same color, pull through, and trim the tail. To start a new thread, either run the needle through the backs of previous stitches in the same color, or begin a new area with the stitch-to-the-knot method.

STEP 4 When all the cross-stitch is complete, add any straight stitches required. These are usually represented on a chart by straight lines. They may run along the lines of holes, or lie diagonally across one or more squares, or be placed on top of cross-stitches. Such lines may be worked in either double running stitch, as here, or backstitch.

STEP 5 When all the stitching is complete, remove the fabric from the hoop or frame and gently pull out the basted center lines.

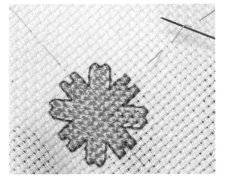

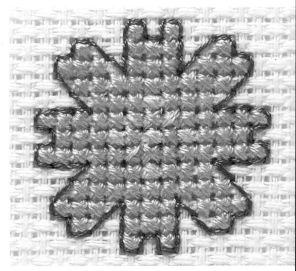

STEP 6 Press the finished embroidery.

WORKING PART-STITCHES

This chart includes part cross-stitches—both three-quarter and quarter—enabling the designer to make a more detailed image.

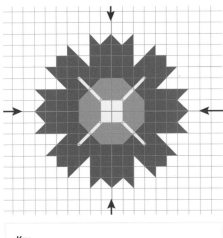

Work the stitching in the same way as above, stitching the part-stitches as they occur. If you prefer, you can stitch all the full crosses first, then go back and add all the part-stitches, but this method is not quite so neat and may require extra thread.

SEE ALSO
Preparing fabric for counted thread work page 14
Mounting in a hoop page 15
Stitch-to-the-knot method page 18
Cross-stitch page 86
Double running stitch page 82
Backstitch page 80
Part cross-stitches page 88
Pressing page 20

KEY

■ Blue cross-stitch	◣ ◳	Blue part stitches
■ Turquoise cross-stitch	◢ ◲	
■ Yellow cross-stitch	◣ ◳	Turquoise part stitches
╲ Yellow straight stitch	◢ ◲	

PROJECT 1 GREETING CARD

Here's a foolproof way to position any embroidered motif in a window card mount so that you can make the perfect greeting card for any occasion.

MATERIALS
- Window card mount: for the small card use 3½ x 4½ in. (9 x 11.5 cm) mount with oval window 2⅜ x 3 in. (6 x 7.5 cm); for the large card use 4 x 6 in. (10 x 15 cm) mount with oval window 2¾ x 3¾ in. (7 x 9.5 cm)
- 14-count Aida fabric in white, at least ¼ in. (6 mm) larger all around than the front of the closed card
- Embroidery hoop or frame
- Six-strand cotton embroidery floss: for the small card approximately 1 yard (1 m) light blue, 1 yard (1 m) green, and ½ yard (0.5 m) dark blue; for the large card approximately 1½ yards (1.5 m) light blue, 2½ yards (2 m) green, and ½ yard (0.5 m) dark blue
- Tapestry needle, size 22 or 24
- Lightweight batting
- Water-soluble fabric pen, tape measure, scissors
- Double-sided tape

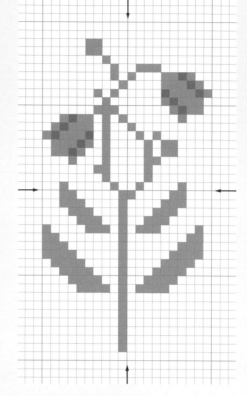

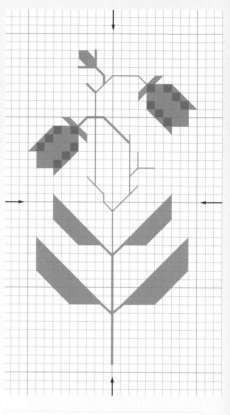

KEY

▓ Green cross-stitch		▓ Dark blue cross-stitch
▓ Light blue cross-stitch		⟋ Green double running stitch

EMBROIDERY NOTES
Choose either the simple cross-stitch version, or the version with part-stitches and double running stitch. Follow the Cross-stitch guidelines on page 27. On 14-count Aida fabric, use two strands of thread throughout. On 10-count Aida fabric use three strands for the cross-stitch and two strands for the double running stitch.

ASSEMBLY INSTRUCTIONS

STEP 1
Lay the embroidery flat and center a card window mount over it. Use a water-soluble fabric pen to mark the size of the card front onto the fabric. Cut the fabric ¼ in. (6 mm) inside the marked lines. Cut the side edges first.

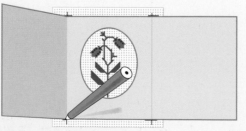

STEP 2
Position the window card mount over some lightweight batting and lightly draw around the inside of the window, trying not to touch the card with the pen. Cut out the batting shape along the marked line. The shape should fit easily inside the window.

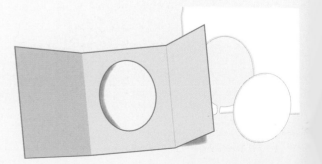

STEP 3 Close the front of the card and place a length of double-sided tape on the inner surface, inside the window. Peel off the backing then position the batting through the window. Press into place with your fingers.

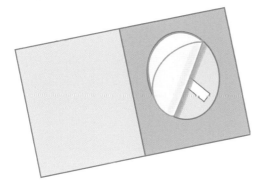

STEP 4 Open up the card. On the inside, place lengths of double-sided tape all around the window. On the inner front, place lengths of tape along the three outer edges.

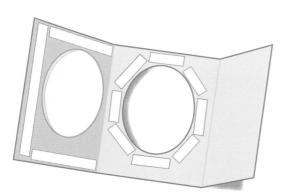

STEP 5 Peel off the backing tape around the window only. Turn the card over and position the window over the embroidery. Do not press down firmly until you are sure the position is correct.

STEP 6 Now peel off the backing tape around the inner front edges. Fold the inner front behind the window and press the edges down firmly.

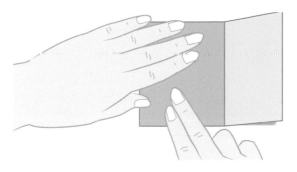

SEE ALSO
Cross-stitch guidelines page 26
Part cross-stitches pages 88–89
Double running stitch page 82

COUNTED STITCHES ON AIDA FABRIC

Besides cross-stitch, many other embroidery stitches can be stitched on Aida fabric by counting the squares from a chart. A cross-stitch design may include a border of other stitches, or the whole design may be worked in counted stitches.

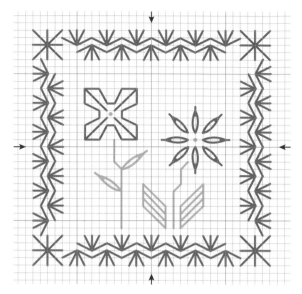

STEP 1 Prepare the Aida fabric for counted thread work and mount it in a hoop or frame. From the table on page 26, select a suitable size of tapestry needle and thickness of floss. Instead of stranded cotton embroidery floss, you can also use a firmer, rounder thread such as perle cotton.

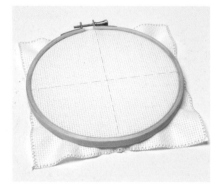

Worked on 11-count Aida fabric, using three strands of embroidery floss, this flower motif will measure 3 in. (7.5 cm) square. On 14-count fabric it will measure about 2½ in. (6 cm) square.

KEY

⌐	Double running stitch
⫽	Satin stitch
∂∂	Single chain stitches
•	French knot
⩔	Fan of 5 straight stitches
◹	Long straight stitches
✳	Algerian eye stitch

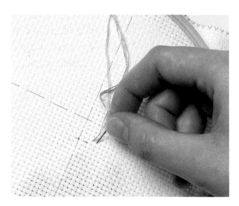

STEP 2 The chart squares correspond with the squares on the fabric in the same way as on a cross-stitch chart. Begin at or near the center of the design to avoid miscounting. Cut 18 in. (50 cm) lengths of thread and divide the strands if necessary. Thread the tapestry needle and start with the waste-knot method.

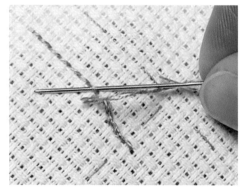

STEP 3 To finish off a thread, run the needle underneath previous stitches on the wrong side of the fabric. Pull through then snip off the remaining thread. Avoid passing the thread across the wrong side from one area to another; instead it is better to fasten off the thread and begin again with another waste knot.

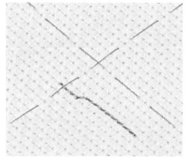

STEP 4 Straight lines of stitches may be worked as backstitch or double running stitch, like the flower stem shown here.

STEP 5 Other arrangements of straight stitches can form part of the design, like this flower petal. Here, some stitches are longer than one square, and some are worked diagonally across two or three squares. For an even appearance, a repeating unit like this petal should be worked in the same order for each repeat.

SEE ALSO
Preparing fabric for counted thread work page 14
Double running stitch page 82
Single chain stitch page 109
French knots page 116
Algerian eye stitch page 94
Satin stitch page 110

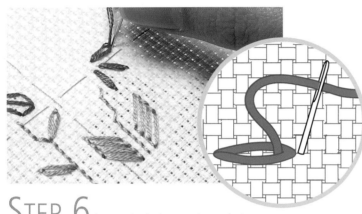

STEP 6 Looped stitches such as chain stitch, blanket stitch, or the single chain stitch shown here are held in place by a final small stitch. Make these small stitches half a square long, either midway between two holes, or at the center of a fabric square.

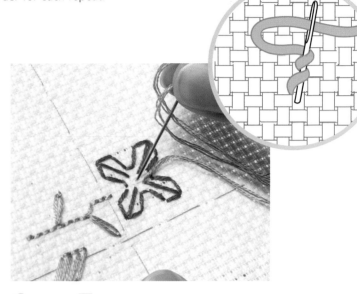

STEP 7 To make a French knot at the center of a square, bring the needle up through a corner hole, then use the needle tip to part the fabric threads at the center of the square. Form the knot in the usual way, inserting the needle through the hole you have made.

STEP 8 Work the border last. As in Step 5, each "fan" of this eyelet pattern border should be worked in the same order for each repeat. It is easier to bring the needle up through an empty hole at the outside of the shape, then take it down through the shared hole at the center. The center hole will enlarge slightly, forming the "eyelet."

STEP 9 When the embroidery is complete, remove it from the frame or hoop. Gently pull out the basted center lines and press the work.

COUNTED STITCHES ON AIDA FABRIC

EVENWEAVE GUIDELINES

Any cross-stitch or other counted thread design can be worked on evenweave fabric instead of Aida. Like Aida, evenweave fabric is woven with an exact number of threads to the inch in each direction, but without an obvious pattern of squares. The stitches are counted over the threads of the weave. Evenweave fabrics are normally available in counts of between 20 and 32 threads per inch, and in a variety of fibers and colors. Their soft handle and washability make them particularly suitable for accessories and projects for the home.

SEE ALSO
Preparing fabric for counted thread work page 14
Cross-stitch guidelines page 26
Cross-stitch page 86
Part cross-stitches pages 88–89

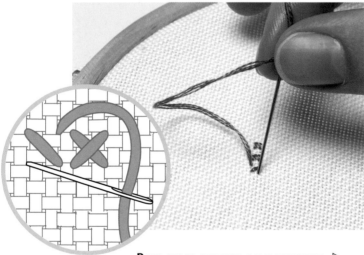

CROSS-STITCH ON EVENWEAVE ◁
Follow the Cross-stitch guidelines on page 26. Each cross-stitch is usually worked over two threads of evenweave in each direction. For example, on 28-count fabric there will be 14 crosses to the inch, the same size as on 14-count Aida fabric. Work each cross-stitch over two threads in each direction.

PART CROSS-STITCHES ON EVENWEAVE ▷
Work part cross-stitches in the same way as on Aida fabric. The long arm of a three-quarter cross-stitch is worked over two threads in each direction (two thread intersections) and the short arm over just one thread intersection.

OTHER COUNTED THREAD STITCHES ON EVENWEAVE
Many other stitches may be counted onto evenweave fabric. In general, one square on a chart will represent two fabric threads in each direction.

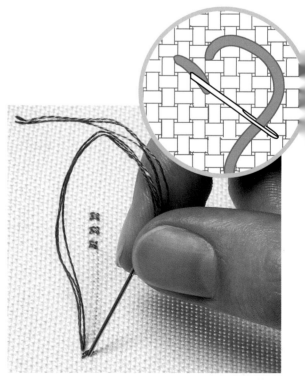

ASSISI WORK

In Assisi work the background is filled with cross-stitch in a solid color and the motif is left unstitched. A decorative border of double running stitch is often added around the outside. It is named after the town of Assisi in Italy, where it developed at the time of the Italian Renaissance.

KEY

■ Blue cross-stitch

⌐ Dark blue double running stitch

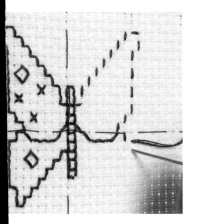

STEP 1
◁ Prepare Aida or evenweave fabric for counted thread work. Use a hoop or frame. Choose a suitable tapestry needle and floss from the table on page 26, and follow the Cross-stitch guidelines on page 26. For the outline of the central motif, choose a dark shade of floss, slightly finer than you would use for cross-stitch—two strands of cotton embroidery floss are shown here. Work the central outline in double running stitch, adding any details inside the shape.

Worked on 11-count Aida fabric, using two strands of embroidery floss for the double running stitch and three strands for the cross-stitch, this butterfly will measure 3 in. (7.5 cm) square. On 14-count Aida, using one and two strands for the embroidery, it will measure about 2½ in. (6 cm) square.

STEP 2
▷ Use a medium shade, heavier floss to fill the background with cross-stitch—three strands of cotton embroidery floss are shown here. It is usually convenient to work these cross-stitches in lines.

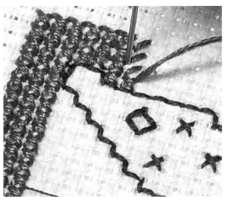

STEP 3
◁ Use the finer dark floss to stitch the outline of the shape and the decorative border in double running stitch.

STEP 4
When stitching is complete, carefully remove the basting lines and press the work. You could mount this butterfly in a greeting card with a square window.

SEE ALSO
Double running stitch page 82
Cross-stitch page 86
Pressing page 20

SCENTED SACHETS

These little sachets can be filled with lavender or potpourri and placed in your closet or dresser.

One is in cross-stitch (with part stitches), and the other in Assisi work.

FINISHED SIZE 2½ x 2½ in.
(6.5 x 6.5 cm)

MATERIALS
- 27-count evenweave fabric in white, 5 x 5 in. (12.5 x 12.5 cm)
- Embroidery hoop or frame
- Six-strand cotton embroidery floss: for cross-stitch version approximately 2 yards (1.8 m) lilac and 1½ yards (1.3 m) yellow; for Assisi work version approximately 2½ yards (2 m) lilac and 1¼ yards (1 m) dark blue
- Tapestry needle, size 22 or 24
- Lightweight backing fabric, such as cotton or silk, 5 x 5 in. (12.5 x 12.5 cm)
- Narrow ribbon, 4 in. (10 cm)
- Sewing equipment: tape measure, scissors, pins, sharp sewing needle, white sewing thread
- Iron
- Blunt knitting needle

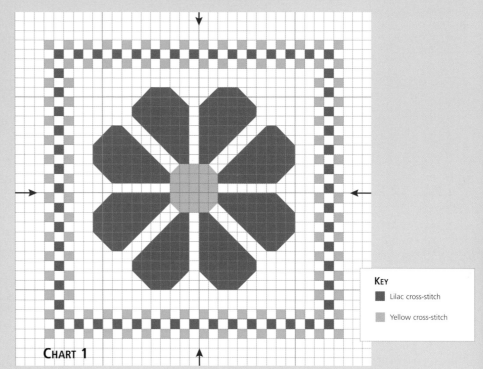

CHART 1

KEY
- ■ Lilac cross-stitch
- ■ Yellow cross-stitch

EMBROIDERY NOTES

For the cross-stitch version, Chart 1, follow the Evenweave guidelines on page 32, using two strands of floss throughout. Work the part cross-stitches as pages 88–89. For the Assisi version, Chart 2, follow the instructions for Assisi work on page 33, using two strands of floss for the cross-stitch and one strand for the double running stitch.

ASSEMBLY INSTRUCTIONS

STEP 1
Measure ½ in. (1.5 cm) outside the edge of the embroidery all around, and trim away the excess fabric following straight lines of holes. Cut a piece of backing fabric to the same size.

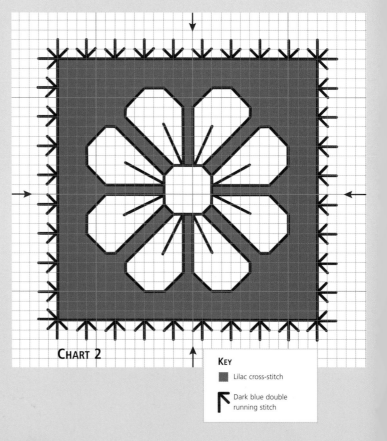

CHART 2

KEY
- ■ Lilac cross-stitch
- ⚹ Dark blue double running stitch

STEP 2
Fold 4 in. (10 cm) of narrow ribbon in half and pin the ends at one corner of the embroidery, on the right side.

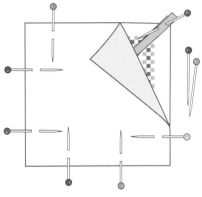

STEP 3
Place the backing fabric and the embroidery with right sides together and pin all around the edges. Use white sewing thread to backstitch or machine stitch ¼ in. (6 mm) outside the edge of the embroidery, following straight lines of holes, and leaving a gap of 1½ in. (4 cm) at the center of one side.

STEP 4
Clip away all four corners, as on page 22, just outside the stitching line, but don't cut through the ends of the ribbon. Press ¼ in. (6 mm) to the wrong side on both edges of the opening.

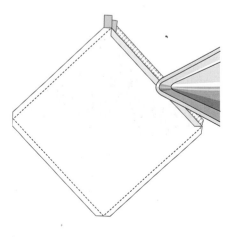

STEP 5
Turn the sachet right side out. Use a knitting needle with a blunt tip, or something similar, to gently push out the corners neatly, then press (see page 22). Fill the sachet with about two teaspoons of dried lavender or potpourri, and pin the opening closed. Use sewing thread and a sharp needle to slipstitch along the opening.

SEE ALSO
Cross-stitch guidelines page 26
Assisi work page 33
Backstitch page 80
Part cross-stitches pages 88–89
Slipstitch page 21
Turning right side out page 22

BLACKWORK

Blackwork is most often stitched in black thread on white or cream Aida fabric or evenweave, although any strongly contrasting colors may be used. Small repeating patterns, usually made with straight stitches, are used to fill different areas of a design. The varying densities of these patterns create different shades when viewed from a distance.

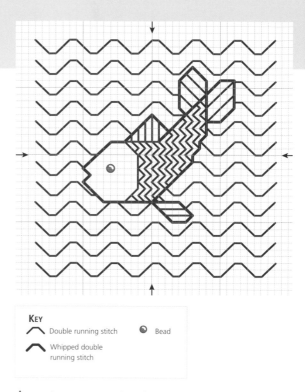

KEY

⌒ Double running stitch   ◕ Bead

⌒ Whipped double running stitch

NOTES

- Where straight stitches are indicated on a blackwork chart you can use either double running stitch or backstitch. Double running stitch usually makes a neater result.
- Blackwork patterns may also be formed with pattern darning, Algerian eye stitch, upright cross-stitch, or star stitch.
- Stitches such as cross-stitch or satin stitch may be used for small, solid areas.
- Details such as eyes may be French knots, small beads, or sequins.

△ *Each square on the chart represents one square of Aida fabric. Straight stitches may be shown stitched along the sides of a square, or diagonally across a square from corner to corner. Some stitch patterns may include longer stitches worked over two or more fabric squares. Worked in perle cotton on 11-count Aida fabric, in double running stitch with a bead for the eye, this fish picture will measure approximately 3 in. (7.5 cm) square.*

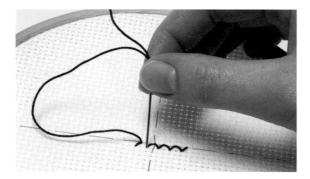

STEP 1
Prepare Aida or evenweave fabric for counted thread work. Choose a tapestry needle to suit your fabric from the table on page 26. Choose a similar weight of floss, or slightly finer. Firm rounded thread, such as perle cotton, gives a clean, bold result, but stranded cotton embroidery floss is also suitable. Begin at or near the center using the waste-knot method. In double running stitch, work one line of pattern out to one edge of the first area, back to the center, then out to the opposite edge and back again to the center. Once you have established the first pattern, fill the whole area following the chart carefully.

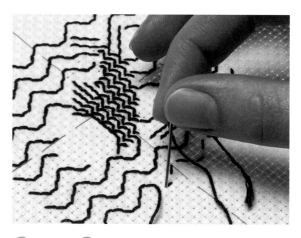

STEP 2
Whatever pattern you are stitching, work each line—or repeating unit—in the same order, to keep the appearance as regular as possible. Patterns may be worked in horizontal, vertical, or diagonal rows, whichever is convenient. Part-stitches may be required at the edges of a shape.

STEP 3 To fasten off a thread, run the end in along the back of previous stitches. To begin another area you can carry the thread across the wrong side, running it along the back of previous stitching. Avoid making long stitches on the wrong side across areas that are lightly stitched or unstitched.

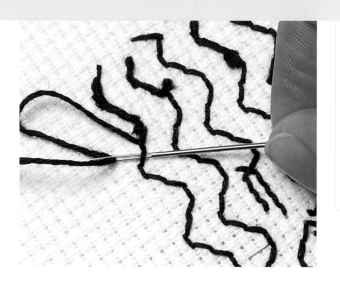

SEE ALSO
Preparing fabric for counted
    thread work page 14
Waste-knot method page 18
Double running stitch page 82
Backstitch page 80
Whipped stitches page 81
Beads, sequins, and special
    threads page 52

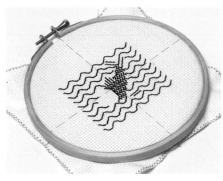

STEP 4 △ Work all the areas of different patterns in this way.

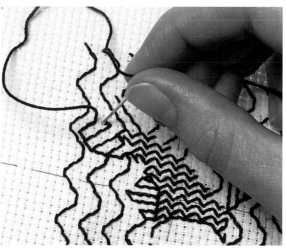

STEP 5 Now stitch the outline around each shape. These outlines are usually worked in double running stitch or backstitch, often with slightly heavier floss.

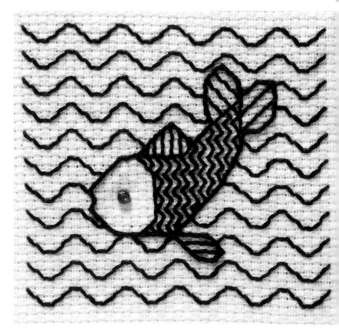

STEP 6 ◁ You can emphasize the outline by whip stitching it with a matching or contrasting thread. This not only makes the outline heavier, but also rounds off any angular corners.

STEP 7 ▷ When all the stitching is complete, sew on any beads or sequins. Remove the work from the hoop or frame and gently pull out the basted center lines. Press the work.

PROJECT 3 POT HOLDER

This decorative pot holder will look wonderful simply hanging in your kitchen, and it has practical uses as well.

FINISHED SIZE 6½ x 6½ in. (16.5 x 16.5 cm)

MATERIALS
- 14-count Aida fabric in white, 8 x 8 in. (20 x 20 cm)
- Embroidery hoop or frame
- Six-stranded cotton embroidery thread: approximately 13½ yards (12 m) dark pink
- Tapestry needle, size 22 or 24
- Backing fabric, such as medium-weight cotton, 7½ x 7½ in. (19 x 19 cm)
- Ribbon, 5 in. (12.5 cm)
- Batting or thermal interlining, 6½ x 6½ in. (16.5 x 16.5 cm)
- Sewing equipment: water-soluble fabric pen, tape measure, scissors, pins, sharp sewing needle, white sewing thread, sewing machine (optional)
- Iron
- Blunt knitting needle or similar implement

EMBROIDERY NOTES
Follow the Blackwork guidelines on page 36. Use two strands of floss for all the stitches on the chart.

KEY

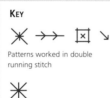

Patterns worked in double running stitch

Algerian eye stitch

ASSEMBLY INSTRUCTIONS

STEP 1 Count 12 squares outside the edge of the embroidery all around, marking the lines lightly with a water-soluble fabric pen, and trim away the excess fabric following straight lines of holes. Cut the backing fabric to exactly the same size.

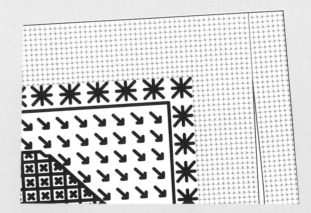

TIP
Blackwork is traditionally worked in black or red thread on white or cream fabric, but you can choose any strong color contrast, such as the bright pink and white used here.

STEP 2
Count and mark six squares outside the edge of the embroidery, on the wrong side, along straight lines of holes. Fold 5 in. (12.5 cm) of ribbon in half and pin the ends at the top corner of the embroidery, on the right side.

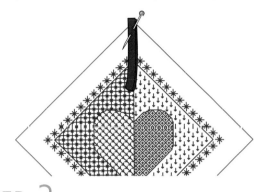

STEP 3
Place the embroidery and the backing fabric with right sides together and pin all around the edges. Use white sewing thread to backstitch or machine stitch along the marked lines, leaving a gap of 3 in. (7.5 cm) at the center of one side.

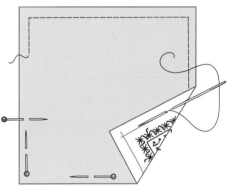

STEP 4
Clip away all four corners, just outside the stitching line, as on page 22, but don't cut through the ends of the ribbon. Press the seam allowances open, and back toward the center, on both sides of the work, all around. Trim some batting or interlining so that it fits neatly under the seam allowances on the embroidered side. Pin it in place then use white sewing thread to baste it in position, stitching through the seam allowance and batting only, not through to the right side of the work.

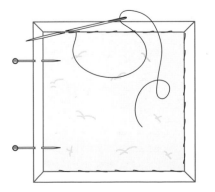

STEP 5
Turn the pot holder right side out. Use a knitting needle with a blunt tip, or something similar, to gently push out the corners. Pin the opening closed. Use sewing thread and a sharp needle to slipstitch along the opening. Press the edges carefully (see page 20).

STEP 6
Using three strands of embroidery floss and a sharp needle, begin to work blanket stitch around the edge of the pot holder. Make the stitches four squares deep and two squares apart. To keep the stitches regular on the wrong side, insert the needle vertically through the holes in the Aida fabric. At each corner you will need to work three stitches into the same place, but after working the second of these three stitches, anchor it in place exactly on the corner with a tiny backstitch before continuing. At the top corner, work through the ribbon with the outer edge of the blanket stitches on top of the ribbon.

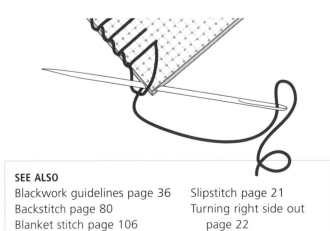

SEE ALSO

Blackwork guidelines page 36   Slipstitch page 21
Backstitch page 80   Turning right side out
Blanket stitch page 106   page 22

Half cross-stitch on canvas

Embroidery on canvas is usually worked to cover the canvas completely, using soft, full threads such as tapestry wool, Persian wool, or soft cotton. Designs may be charted, or printed on the canvas.

SEE ALSO
Basting center lines page 14
Handling skeins of floss page 17
Threading needles page 17
Stitch-to-the-knot method page 18
Half cross-stitch page 85
Blocking page 20

TABLE OF SUITABLE THREADS AND NEEDLES FOR CANVAS

From the table below, choose a size of tapestry needle and thread to suit your canvas. Threads given are suitable for half cross-stitch or other diagonal stitches on canvas.

Single canvas mesh	Tapestry needle size	Strands of Persian wool	Other suitable threads
10-count	18	3	Tapestry wool
12-count	20	2	Tapestry wool
14-count	20	2	Soft cotton embroidery thread
18-count	22	1	

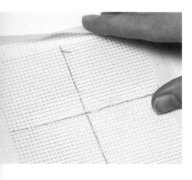

STEP 1
Cut the canvas along straight lines of holes, at least 1 in. (2.5 cm) larger all around than the finished embroidery. Small canvas embroideries may be worked without a frame or hoop, if they are small enough to hold in the hand without crumpling. Draw the center lines along straight lines of canvas holes with a water-soluble fabric pen. Bind the raw edges with masking tape to prevent the canvas catching the thread as you stitch. Larger embroideries are best mounted in a frame.

STEP 2
Begin at or near the center using the stitch-to-the-knot method. Use lengths of thread no longer than 18 in. (45 cm), to prevent fraying. Each square on the chart represents one half cross-stitch worked on the canvas mesh. Work back and forth in rows to fill each area of color.

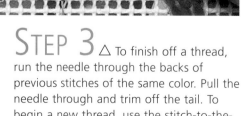

STEP 3
△ To finish off a thread, run the needle through the backs of previous stitches of the same color. Pull the needle through and trim off the tail. To begin a new thread, use the stitch-to-the-knot method, or run the thread in along the back of previous stitches of the same color.

STEP 4
When complete, remove the masking tape, or take the embroidery out of the frame. Mist with water and block the work. This strawberry motif was used for the book cover, opposite.

BOOK COVER

Make a cover for a diary, address book, or recipe book with a simple needlepoint panel.

MATERIALS

- 12-count evenweave tapestry canvas 3 x 3 in. (7.5 x 7.5 cm)
- Tapestry wool: approximately 2 yards (1.8 m) strawberry red, 3 yards (3.6 m) soft yellow, and 10 in. (25 cm) green
- Tapestry needle, size 18
- Book, 6 x 4 in. (15 x 10 cm), or as required
- Felt, to fit book
- Sewing equipment: water-soluble fabric pen, tape measure, scissors, pins, sharp sewing needle, sewing thread for basting
- Ruler and set square
- Sharp needle, similar size to tapestry needle
- Perle cotton: approximately 8 yards (7.2 m) to complement strawberry red

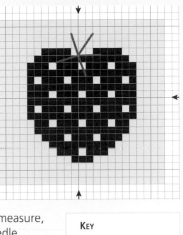

EMBROIDERY NOTES

Follow the Half cross-stitch on canvas guidelines on page 40. First work all the red half cross-stitches, then the yellow ones. Work the green straight stitches over the top.

ASSEMBLY INSTRUCTIONS

STEP 1 Measure the book with a tape measure, as

shown below. Use a ruler, set square, and water-soluble fabric pen to draw the outlines onto the felt, matching your measurements and adding ¼ in. (6 mm) seam allowances as shown. To ensure your drawing is accurately square, the two diagonals a–a' and b–b' should both measure exactly the same. Draw the 2 x 2 in. (5 x 5 cm) window: ours is at the center of the front panel, 1¼ in. (3 cm) from the top. Cut out the pieces.

STEP 2 Pin the embroidery

behind the window, matching the edges carefully. Baste all around with sewing thread. Use a sharp needle and perle cotton to work blanket stitch all around the edge of the window, covering the raw edge of the felt. Use the canvas mesh beneath to keep the stitches an even size: ours were two holes deep and two holes apart. At each corner, work three stitches in the same place. Remove the basting.

STEP 3 Pin the cover in

position with the book closed. Baste the edges together all around. Use the sharp needle and perle cotton to work blanket stitch all around the outside edge, through both layers of felt, matching the size of the stitches to those around the window. Work three stitches into the same place at each corner. Hide the thread ends between the felt layers. Remove the basting. Mist with water to remove traces of the water-soluble fabric pen and allow to dry.

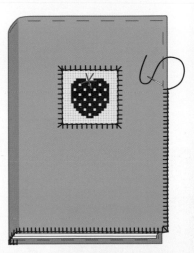

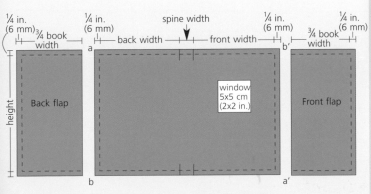

¼ in. (6 mm) ¾ book width   ¼ in. (6 mm) ← back width →   spine width ↓ ← front width →   ¼ in. (6 mm) ¾ book width   ¼ in. (6 mm)

a   b'

Back flap   window 5x5 cm (2x2 in.)   Front flap

height

b   a'

CANVASWORK GUIDELINES

Many counted thread stitches can be worked on canvas. Suitable threads include Persian wool, tapestry wool, and soft cotton. Canvaswork stitches normally cover the canvas completely.

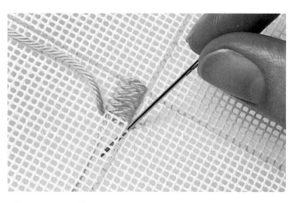

TESTING THREAD COVERAGE

Use the same canvas and needle as you intend to use for the project, and try out a few stitches to see how they look.

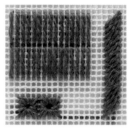

On 14-count canvas, one strand of Persian wool is too thin: the vertical satin stitch shows gaps between the stitches, although the slanting stitches cover the canvas better.

Two strands of Persian wool give much better coverage, making solid blocks of color.

Worked on 14-count canvas in four colors of soft cotton embroidery thread, this patchwork square measures 2½ in. (5.5 cm) square. On 12-count or 10-count canvas it would measure about 2⅝ in. (6.5 cm) or 3 in. (7.5 cm) square, and heavier thread such as three strands of Persian wool, or tapestry wool, would be required.

STEP 1 Prepare the canvas following Step 1 of Half cross-stitch on canvas and choose a tapestry needle from the table on page 40. The threads quoted in this table are suitable for slanting or diagonal stitches, but for stitches worked parallel with the canvas mesh choose slightly heavier thread. It is usually best to work in a frame, although small pieces can be held in the hand.

STEP 2 Cut thread lengths of no more than about 18 in. (45 cm). Stranded Persian wool should be divided in the same way as stranded embroidery floss, then recombined if necessary. Each intersection on the chart grid corresponds with a hole in the canvas. Begin at or near the center of the canvas using the stitch-to-the-knot method.

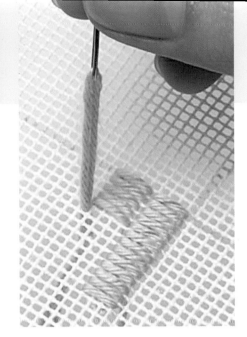

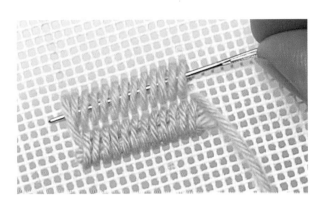

STEP 3
Try to plan a logical order for your stitching: it is easier to bring the needle up through an empty hole than through a hole that is already crowded, although sometimes this is unavoidable.

STEP 4
To fasten off a thread, run the needle through the back of previous stitches for about 1 in. (2.5 cm) then pull it through and snip the thread. When passing threads across the back from one area to another, run the needle along the back of previous stitches in the same way, to avoid long loops. Begin new threads by running along the back of previous stitches of the same color, or stitch-to-the-knot, whichever is more convenient.

TIPS
1. If the thread knots up and is difficult to stitch with, you have probably threaded the needle with the "rough" end of the thread. See page 17.
2. If the thread twists up as you stitch, stop every few stitches and twirl the needle between your fingers to untwist it. If it untwists, twirl the needle in the other direction.

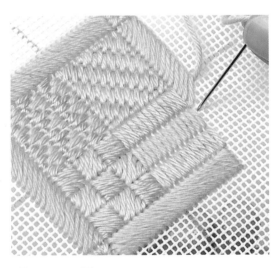

STEP 5
△ Work out from the center, stitching the outside border last.

STEP 6
▷ When the canvaswork is complete, remove it from the frame (if used) and pull off the masking tape. Mist with water to remove traces of water-soluble fabric pen. Canvaswork may require blocking to shape.

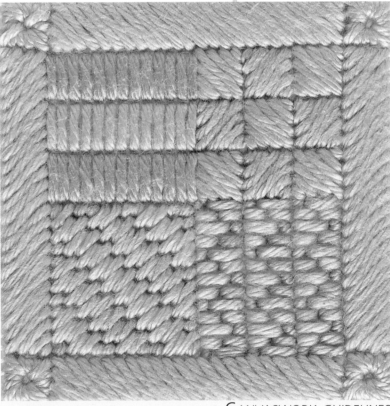

PHOTO FRAME

Stitch this canvaswork frame in any color combination to show off your favorite photograph.

FINISHED SIZE 10½ x 8½ in. (26.5 x 21.5 cm), to fit 6 x 4 in. (15 x 10 cm) photograph

MATERIALS

- Photograph, 6 x 4 in. (15 x 10 cm)
- 12-count evenweave tapestry canvas, 13 x 11 in. (33 x 28 cm)
- Embroidery frame
- Tapestry wool: approximately 25 yards (23 m) cornflower blue, 17 yards (16 m) jade green, 20 yards (18.5 m) turquoise, and 10 yards (9.5 m) pale turquoise
- Tapestry needle, size 20
- Felt for backing in blue, 10½ x 8½ in. (26.5 x 21.5 cm)
- Narrow ribbon, 4 in. (10 cm)
- Sewing equipment: scissors, pins, sharp sewing needle, blue sewing thread to match felt
- Iron and damp cloth
- Fabric glue and spatula
- Thick cardboard, 10¼ x 8¼ in. (26 x 21 cm)
- Clear acetate sheet, 10¼ x 8¼ in. (26 x 21 cm)
- Pen
- Double-sided tape

EMBROIDERY NOTES

Do not cut the canvas to size until the embroidery is complete.
Follow the Canvaswork guidelines on page 42. The first corner (top left) of the frame is worked exactly as on the chart. The top right corner is a mirror image of the first corner, and the bottom half is a mirror image of the top half. However, the top threads of the cross-stitches should lie all in the same direction, and the diagonal directions of the cushion stitches (satin stitch blocks) should be consistent throughout.
Begin by working the edging all around the inner rectangle (green blanket stitches of varying length, with satin stitches at the corners). Then work each successive border of stitches all around, ending at the outer edge.

ASSEMBLY INSTRUCTIONS

STEP 1
When the embroidery is complete, cut the canvas along the cutting lines indicated on the chart. Snip across each outer corner. At each inner corner, carefully snip into the corner.

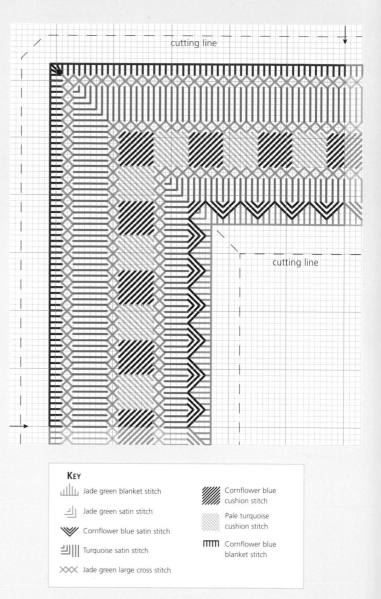

cutting line

cutting line

KEY

⊥⊥⊥⊥ Jade green blanket stitch	⧄ Cornflower blue cushion stitch
⌐ Jade green satin stitch	⧄ Pale turquoise cushion stitch
⩔ Cornflower blue satin stitch	⊓⊓⊓ Cornflower blue blanket stitch
⌐⏐⏐ Turquoise satin stitch	
✕✕✕ Jade green large cross stitch	

STEP 2
Press all the unstitched edges to the wrong side, using a warm iron and a damp cloth. Make neat folds at the outer corners. From the right side, no empty canvas should be visible.

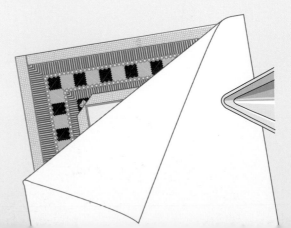

STEP 3
Spread a little fabric glue along the inner raw edges and use a spatula or small piece of cardboard to press the canvas thread ends down onto the back of the embroidery, especially at the corners where the thread ends are very short. Don't use too much glue or it may soak through to the front. Allow to dry.

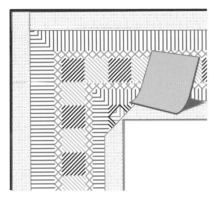

STEP 4
The cardboard and acetate sheet should both be about ⅛ in. (3 mm) smaller all around than the embroidered frame. Center the frame over the cardboard and slip the photograph under the window. The window is slightly smaller than 6 x 4 in. (15 x 10 cm), so you have a little leeway to adjust the position of the photograph. Carefully lift the frame away and mark the position of the corners of the photograph on the cardboard. Apply four small pieces of double-sided tape inside the marked corners, peel away the backing tape, and replace the photograph, matching the corner marks. Then apply four more pieces of tape to the outer corners of the cardboard, peel away the backing tape, and fix the acetate sheet in place.

STEP 5
Fold the ribbon in half and pin the two ends to the wrong side of the frame at the center of one short edge. Use sewing thread to slipstitch the ends in place to the back of the embroidery stitches.

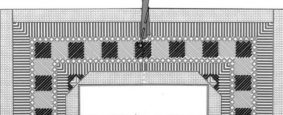

STEP 6
Pin blue felt to the back of the frame all around the edge. Use the blue sewing thread to slipstitch around three sides, leaving the top edge open. Stitch the edge of the felt to the back of the blanket stitch edging.

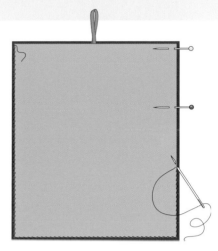

STEP 7
Slip the mounted photograph inside the frame and slipstitch along the top edge.

SEE ALSO

Canvaswork guidelines
   page 42
Blanket stitch page 106
Mounting in a frame page 16
Slipstitch page 21

Cross-stitch guidelines
   page 26
Satin stitch (and cushion
   stitch) page 110

USING WASTE CANVAS

This technique is used to work designs in counted thread stitches onto plain fabric. Our example is worked in cross-stitch and star stitch, but other counted thread stitches may be worked in the same way.

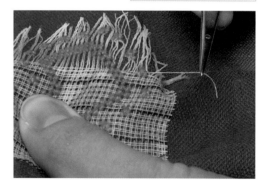

Worked over 14-count waste canvas, in cross-stitch (page 86) and star stitch (page 91), this motif measures 2 x 2 in. (5 x 5 cm).

KEY
- ■ Cross-stitch
- ✳ Star stitch

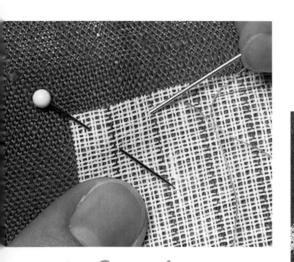

STEP 1
Cut waste canvas at least 1 in. (2.5 cm) larger all around than the finished motif, along straight lines of holes. Baste the center lines (see page 14). Pin the waste canvas where required on the plain fabric and use a sharp needle and sewing thread to baste all around, about ¼ in. (6 mm) in from the raw edges. For a large piece of waste canvas, add more basting to form a grid of 4 in. (10 cm) squares.

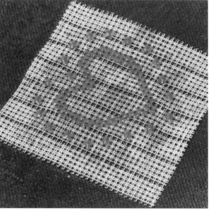

STEP 2
Mount the fabric in a hoop or frame. Use a sharp needle to work the embroidery, counting each square on the chart as one square of waste canvas. Do not split canvas threads or basting stitches with the sharp needle. When the embroidery is complete, take it out of the hoop or frame. Pull out the basting. Cut away excess canvas, a few squares outside the embroidery. Mist with water to soften the waste canvas.

STEP 3
Use tweezers to gently pull out all the canvas threads in one direction, one by one. Then pull out all the canvas threads in the other direction.

STEP 4
Allow to dry, then press the work.

NOTES
- The threads of the special waste canvas are treated with water-soluble glue, so that when the canvas is moistened, it can be easily pulled apart.
- Some plain fabrics, such as silks, are susceptible to water-staining. If in doubt, test a scrap of fabric by misting it with water and allowing it to dry.
- Waste canvas is normally available only in 14-count, so three strands of cotton embroidery floss are suitable for cross-stitch.

HEART NAPKIN

This napkin matches the pot holder on page 38—make as many as you want.

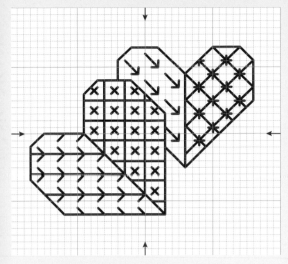

STEP 2 Work the blackwork from the chart, following the waste canvas guidelines on page 46, Steps 2–4.

STEP 3 Press the embroidery right side down on a well-padded surface. Fold and press ¼ in. (6 mm) to the wrong side all around. Then fold and press an additional ½ in. (12 mm) all around, arranging the corners neatly. Pin the hem in place and hemstitch all around with white sewing thread (see page 23).

FINISHED SIZE 18 x 18 in. (45 x 45 cm)

MATERIALS
• Plain cotton or linen fabric in white, 19½ x 19½ in. (49 x 49 cm)
• Waste canvas, 4 x 4 in. (10 x 10 cm)
• Embroidery hoop
• Six-strand cotton embroidery floss: approximately 2½ yards (2.3 m) dark pink
• Crewel needle, size 7
• Sewing equipment: water-soluble fabric pen, tape measure, scissors, pins, sharp sewing needle, white sewing thread, contrasting sewing thread, sewing machine (optional)
• Tweezers
• Iron

EMBROIDERY NOTES
Follow the Blackwork guidelines on page 36. Use two strands of thread for all the stitches on the chart.

ASSEMBLY INSTRUCTIONS

STEP 1 Overcast or machine zigzag with white sewing thread all around the edges of the cotton or linen fabric to prevent fraying. Baste center lines onto the waste canvas using contrasting sewing thread. Pin the waste canvas at one corner of the fabric, on the right side, 2 in. (5 cm) in from the edges. Baste around the edge of the waste canvas.

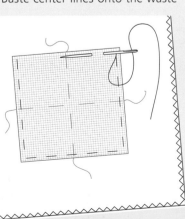

SEE ALSO
Blackwork guidelines page 36
Basting center lines page 14
Mounting in a hoop page 15
Waste canvas guidelines page 46
Turning hems page 23

Hardanger work

Hardanger work is named for the district in Norway where it originated. Geometric designs are formed by securing threads with blocks of satin stitch (called Kloster blocks), then cutting and drawing out certain threads to leave a grid, which may be decorated in various ways with "bars" and "fillings" to form intricate patterns.

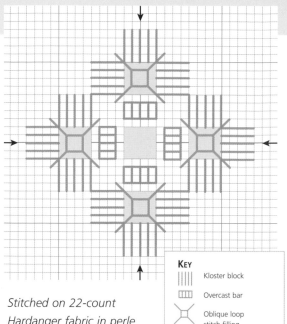

Stitched on 22-count Hardanger fabric in perle cotton Nos. 5 and 8, this motif measures 1¼ in. (3 cm) square. On 18-count fabric it would measure about 1⅝ in. (3.7 cm) square, and on 25-count evenweave fabric, about 1 in. (2.5 cm) square.

KEY

|||||	Kloster block
▯▯▯▯	Overcast bar
⊠	Oblique loop stitch filling

SUITABLE THREADS AND NEEDLES FOR HARDANGER WORK

A firm, rounded thread such as perle cotton gives the best results with Hardanger work. Threads of two thicknesses are used, the heavier thread for the Kloster blocks and the finer thread for the bars and fillings. You can substitute other threads of equivalent thicknesses.

Fabric	Heavier thread: perle cotton	Lighter thread: perle cotton	Tapestry needle sizes
18-count Hardanger	No. 3	No. 5	20 and 22
20-count Hardanger	No. 5	No. 8	22 and 24
22-count Hardanger	No. 5	No. 8	22 and 24
25-count evenweave	No. 5	No. 8	24 and 26
27-count evenweave	No. 5	No. 8	24 and 26
32-count evenweave	No. 8	No. 12	24 and 26

NOTES

- Traditionally, Hardanger work is stitched in white thread on white linen. You can choose other colors, but a close match between fabric and threads gives the neatest appearance.
- Fabrics are specially woven for Hardanger work, the threads being smooth and easy to withdraw. Evenweave fabrics are also suitable for finer work.

STEP 1
Prepare the fabric for counted thread work and mount in a hoop or frame. Use colored sewing thread to baste the outline of the design in small running stitches, indicating accurately the outside edge of the motif.

STEP 2
Use the heavier thread and larger tapestry needle to work the Kloster blocks around the area where threads will be cut and withdrawn. Begin with the waste-knot method at one corner of the shape and work clockwise around it. Make sure you match the direction of the stitches to the chart. Always bring the needle up through the fabric on the outer edge and insert it on the inner edge of each block. Avoid passing the thread across the back of unstitched fabric.

SEE ALSO
Preparing fabric for counted
   thread work page 14
Running stitch page 84
Kloster blocks page 96
Satin stitch page 110
Overcast bars page 97
Oblique loop stitch filling
   page 101

STEP 3
Some designs may include other satin stitch elements outside the main motif. If so, work these next with the same needle and thread. Gently pull out the basted center lines and outline. Secure each thread end along the back of four or five blocks.

STEP 4
Use small, sharp embroidery scissors for cutting threads. At the base of a block, inside the shape, cut through those threads that run in the same direction as the stitches. For each Kloster block of five stitches, there will be four double threads to cut. Cut each thread in turn, very carefully, as close as possible to the stitches: insert the scissor point under a double thread and bring the point out again before closing the scissors. Then cut through the same four threads at the base of the opposite Kloster block. Work around the shape until all the required threads have been cut.

STEP 5
Use tweezers to gently pull out the cut threads. First pull out all the cut threads in one direction, one by one. Then pull out all the cut threads in the opposite direction, leaving a grid of uncut threads.

STEP 6
Use the finer thread and smaller needle to work the bars and fillings. It is best to begin in one corner and work diagonally up and down the design. Here, the bars are being overcast before adding the fillings.

STEP 7
Work the filling stitches last. Press the embroidery when complete.

PROJECT 7   TRINKET BOX

A Hardanger star makes a lovely motif for this ceramic trinket box.

FINISHED SIZE to fit box with 3½ in. (89 mm) diameter lid

MATERIALS

• Ceramic trinket box with 3½ in. (89 mm) lid, designed for mounting embroidery
• 22-count Hardanger fabric in white, 5 x 5 in. (12.5 x 12.5 cm) or larger to fit hoop
• Embroidery hoop
• Perle cotton thread size 5: approximately 4 yards (3.5 m) white
• Perle cotton thread size 8: approximately 3 yards (2.8 m) white, or substitute 1 yard (0.9 m) stranded cotton embroidery floss
• Tapestry needles, sizes 22 and 24
• Backing fabric, such as medium-weight silk, 5 x 5 in. (12.5 x 12.5 cm)
• Sewing equipment: water-soluble fabric pen, very small sharp scissors, sharp sewing needle, white sewing thread, contrasting sewing thread
• Iron
• Anti-fray solution

EMBROIDERY NOTES

Hardanger work is traditionally stitched in white (or cream) thread on white (or cream) fabric. Choose any contrasting color for the backing fabric, to suit the color of your box. You can also choose a different color for the thread. This makes the stitches easier to see, but if the thread color is a strong contrast, the ends of the cut threads will be noticeable. Choose a pastel shade for white or cream fabric. Follow the Hardanger guidelines on page 48.

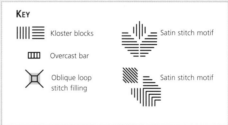

KEY

‖‖‖ Kloster blocks		Satin stitch motif
▥ Overcast bar		
✕ Oblique loop stitch filling		Satin stitch motif

ASSEMBLY INSTRUCTIONS

STEP 1
Baste the center lines on the Hardanger fabric using contrasting sewing thread. Mount the fabric in an embroidery hoop. Baste the design outline, then use the size 5 perle cotton to work all the Kloster blocks clockwise as shown.

STEP 2
Use the same thread to work all the satin stitch motifs around the edge. Between motifs, pass the thread along the wrong side of the Kloster blocks.

STEP 3
Snip the threads at the base of each Kloster block and draw the loose threads. Use perle cotton size 8 (or two strands of stranded cotton embroidery floss) for the rest of the embroidery. Stitch the overcast bars beginning at one corner and working diagonally across the center diamond in the order shown. Overcast each bar seven times and, where necessary, pass the thread along the wrong side of the Kloster blocks between one diagonal row and the next.

STEP 4
Using the same thread, work the oblique loop stitch fillings in a similar order, passing the thread along the wrong side of the Kloster blocks and overcast bars between the squares.

STEP 5
Remove the basted center lines. Press the finished embroidery right side down on a well-padded surface. Center the metal rim of the trinket box lid over the embroidery and draw carefully around the outside edge of the lid with a water-soluble fabric pen. Cut out the circle just inside the marked line. Mist with water to remove any traces of fabric pen and allow to dry.

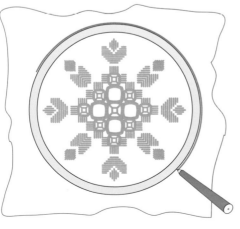

STEP 6
Coat the cut edge with a little anti-fray solution and allow to dry again. Pin the embroidery right side up on the backing fabric. If the backing fabric has a noticeable grain, match it to the grain on the embroidery. Use sewing thread to baste all around, close to the outside edge, then cut the backing to match the embroidery. Mount the embroidery in the box lid as instructed by the manufacturer.

SEE ALSO
Hardanger work page 48
Basting center lines page 14
Mounting in a hoop page 15
Cutting and drawing threads page 49
Oblique loop stitch filling page 101
Overcast bars page 97
Satin stitch page 110

BEADS AND SEQUINS

All kinds of beads, sequins, and special threads can be used to add sparkle to your work. For a really glamorous look, you can stitch a whole project in lurex threads with beads and shiny sequins.

BEADS
Tiny beads can be obtained in a wide range of colors and finishes, such as glassy, pearlized, and fluorescent. These are often used to add details to a cross-stitch design, or a charted motif may be worked entirely in beads, stitching one bead to each fabric square.

BEADS OVER SQUARES
To position a bead over an Aida fabric square, bring the needle up at one corner, thread the bead onto the needle, then pass the needle down at the opposite corner.

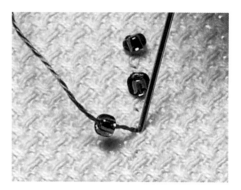

BEADS OVER HOLES
To position a bead over an Aida fabric hole, bring the needle up through the hole, thread on the bead, and take the needle down again through the same hole.

SEQUINS
Sequins are flat shapes— often circular—cut from metallic foil, with a center hole. They can be stitched onto fabric in various ways. Sequins may be added to any embroidery, whether counted thread or freestyle. They are shown here on plain fabric.

SECURING ROWS OF SEQUINS
A line of sequins may be secured with backstitches. Bring the needle up where required, pass it through the hole in a sequin, and hold the sequin down on the fabric. Then make a backstitch across to one side of the sequin. Careful spacing is required to make a neat line.

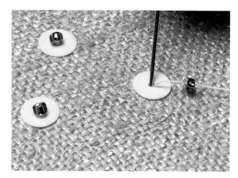

SECURING SINGLE SEQUINS
This method secures sequins without any visible threads. Bring the needle up through the fabric, thread on a sequin and a tiny bead, then pass the needle back through the sequin hole. Make a tiny backstitch on the wrong side of the fabric behind the sequin, then pass the thread across the wrong side to the next position.

SPECIAL THREADS

Special threads such as metallic (lurex), shiny rayon, or fluorescent threads can be tricky to handle. Some special threads are designed to be used alone and may be substituted for stranded cotton embroidery floss of a similar thickness. Other special threads, called blending filaments, are very fine and are usually combined with one or two strands of embroidery floss.

SEE ALSO
Threading needles page 17
Backstitch page 80

NOTES
- Choose a needle one or two sizes larger than you would use for a similar thickness of stranded cotton embroidery floss (see the table on page 26). This will enlarge the hole slightly and prevent metallic threads from fraying as they pass through the fabric.
- Work only with short lengths of thread, no more than 18 in. (45 cm).

LOCKING FINE THREAD ONTO THE NEEDLE
Any thread that is very fine or slippery may be locked onto the needle to make stitching easier. To combine blending filament with another thread, lock the filament onto the needle then thread the second thread in the usual way. Keep both threads the same length as you stitch to avoid knots.

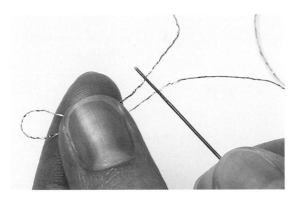

STEP 2 ▷ Pass the needle tip through the loop.

STEP 1 △ Double the thread about 3 in. (7.5 cm) from the end and pass the loop through the needle eye.

◁ **THREADING HEAVY THREADS**
Braids and ribbons are sometimes too wide to thread easily by the usual method, even into a fairly large needle. Fold a small strip of paper and push the fold through the needle eye. Place the thread end between the paper layers and gently push the paper through, carrying the thread with it.

STEP 3 △ Pull both ends gently to tighten the loop at the end of the eye.

▷ **MOISTENING TWISTED THREAD**
Metallic thread supplied on a spool is often twisted and will tend to knot as you stitch. Run the thread lightly across a damp sponge. Only a slight amount of moisture is required to relax the thread.

SPARKLY BEADED PURSE

Make this little purse as a present, perhaps to "gift-wrap" jewelry or perfume. Or stitch it for yourself, choosing colors to match a special outfit.

FINISHED SIZE 6 x 6 in. (15 x 15 cm)

MATERIALS
• 28-count evenweave fabric in ice blue, 8 x 14 in. (20 x 35 cm)
• Embroidery hoop or frame
• Four-stranded rayon embroidery thread: approximately 39 in. (1 m) each of turquoise and medium-blue
• Tapestry needle, size 22 or 24
• Lining fabric, such as lightweight silk or cotton, 8 x 14 in. (20 x 35 cm)
• 16 silver sequins
• 60 small silver beads
• Narrow braid, cord, or ribbon in silver, approximately 50 in. (1.3 m)
• Sewing equipment: scissors, pins, fine sharp sewing needle to fit through beads, sewing threads to match fabrics, sewing machine (optional)
• Iron
• Blunt knitting needle or similar implement

EMBROIDERY NOTES

The embroidery is not worked at the center of the fabric (see Step 1, this page). One square on this chart represents two threads of evenweave fabric in each direction. Follow the Evenweave guidelines on page 32.

Use a tapestry needle for the embroidered stitches. Use two strands of medium-blue rayon to work the trail of modified Algerian eye stitches and cross-stitches. Use two strands of turquoise rayon to work the modified Algerian eye stitches surrounded by French knots with tails. You may find it helpful to lock this rayon thread onto the needle.

Use a fine sharp needle and sewing thread to sew on the silver beads, and the sequins attached with beads.

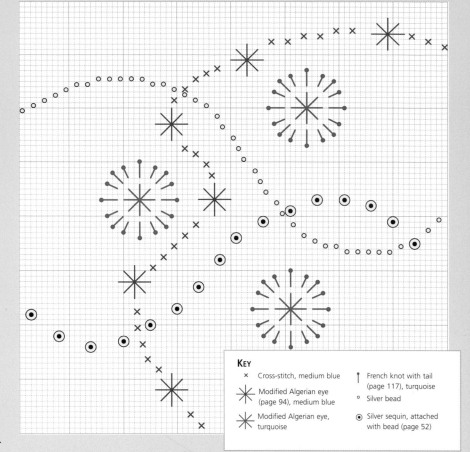

KEY

×	Cross-stitch, medium blue	⸸	French knot with tail (page 117), turquoise
✳	Modified Algerian eye (page 94), medium blue	∘	Silver bead
✳	Modified Algerian eye, turquoise	⊙	Silver sequin, attached with bead (page 52)

ASSEMBLY INSTRUCTIONS

STEP 1
Fold the evenweave fabric in half, matching the short sides, and press the fold line. This fold will be at the base of the finished purse. Measure 3 in. (7.5 cm) up from this line and run a line of basting along a straight row of holes. Fold the fabric in the other direction, matching the long sides, and run another basting line along this fold, from the center to the top edge. Where the two lines cross marks the center of the purse front. Mount the fabric in an embroidery hoop or frame and stitch the embroidery.

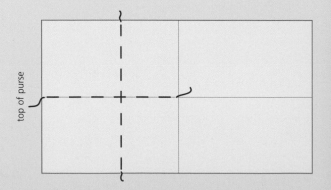

TIP
If your fabric is too small for your hoop or frame, baste strips of waste fabric to the edges as on page 46.

STEP 2
The seam allowance throughout is ⅝ in. (1.5 cm). Fold the completed embroidery in half with right sides together, pin along the seams, then backstitch or machine stitch the seams with matching sewing thread. Stitch from the embroidered side following the straight grain of the fabric. Clip across the two lower corners.

STEP 3
Press the seams open, folding the seam allowances back on each side. Press the seam allowance to the wrong side all around the top opening. Make the lining to match the outer purse, as Steps 2 and 3.

STEP 4
Cut 30 in. (75 cm) of silver braid for the handle. Cut the remaining braid in half for the two ties. Pin the ends of the handle to the outer purse at the tops of the side seams. Pin one end of each tie at the center of the top edge, front and back. Use matching thread to stitch the ends in place, stitching only to the seam allowance, not through to the right side of the purse. Make an overhand knot at the free end of each tie.

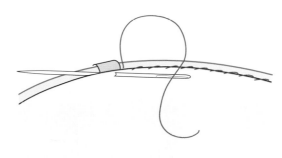

STEP 5
Turn the outer purse right side out. Use a knitting needle with a blunt tip, or something similar, to push out the lower corners neatly (see page 22). Press. Slip the lining inside, with wrong sides together, matching the seams. Pin all around the top edge, with the lining about ⅛ in. (3 mm) below the edge of the outer purse.

STEP 6
Slipstitch by hand around the top edge using sewing thread to match the lining.

SEE ALSO
Cross-stitch guidelines page 26
Mounting in a hoop or frame page 15
Basting center lines page 14
Beads and sequins page 52
Algerian eye stitch page 94
Backstitch page 80
French knots with tails page 117
Slipstitch page 21
Turning right side out page 22

freestyle
embroidery

Freestyle or "surface" embroidery may be worked on many different types of fabric. The stitches are not counted onto the fabric weave, but follow a traced or transferred design. Flowing lines and natural forms can be rendered using a wide variety of stitches and threads on almost any fabric.

TRACING DESIGNS

Use this simple technique to trace a design outline onto light- or medium-weight fabric, then embroider with the colors and stitches of your choice.

KEY

- ⟍ Single chain stitch
- ◦ French knot
- ᛦ French knot with tail
- Y Fly stitch
- ⋮ Chain stitch
- ☀ Circle of blanket stitch

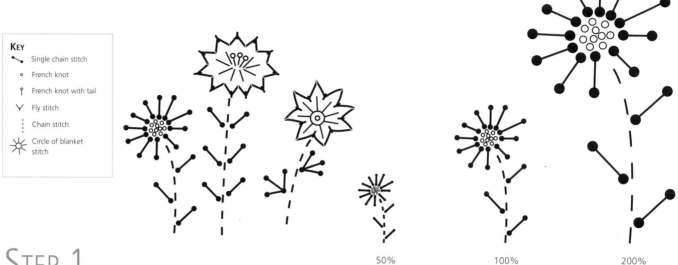

50%   100%   200%

STEP 1
Begin with a clear outline drawing on lightweight paper—photocopy paper is fine—or tracing paper.

STEP 2
If necessary, reduce or enlarge the drawing by photocopying it. If you photocopy a picture at 50%, the size will be halved in each direction. If you photocopy at 200%, the size will be doubled in each direction. Most modern photocopiers allow a wide range of percentages for reduction or enlargement.

STEP 3
Tape the full-size design to a lightbox.

STEP 4
Tape the fabric over the design, then use a water-soluble fabric pen to trace the design lines onto the fabric. The fabric is now ready for embroidery.

IMPROVISE A LIGHTBOX

If you don't have a lightbox, you can improvise with a sheet of glass or Lucite supported on bricks or books over a table lamp. Alternatively, you can tape your design and fabric to a sunny windowpane.

TIPS
- If you are working from a picture not designed specifically for embroidery, make a tracing of the outline and any details you want to include.
- You can also reduce or enlarge a picture with a computer and scanner.
- If the lines of an enlarged image are fuzzy, make a new tracing with sharp, clear lines.

FREESTYLE EMBROIDERY GUIDELINES

When you have traced your design onto fabric,

you are ready to stitch.

SUITABLE NEEDLES AND THREADS
This is only an approximate guide. Choose the smallest needle that will carry the chosen thread easily through the fabric. You can substitute other threads of equivalent thickness to the strands quoted here.

Fabric weight	Sharp needle size	Strands of cotton embroidery floss
Light, such as fine cottons and silks	Crewel size 7–10	1 or 2
Medium, such as linen, calico cotton, and silk dupion	Crewel size 3–6	3 or 4
Heavy, such as coarse linen and wool	Chenille size 13-18	6 or more

STEP 1 Prepare the fabric for freestyle embroidery and mount it in a frame or hoop. If possible, choose a hoop large enough to take the whole design.

STEP 2 Choose a suitable needle and weight of thread from the table on the left. You may wish to use a thimble. You can try out a few stitches in one corner to make sure you like the result. You can begin anywhere, but it is often a good idea to start with the background, so that when you stitch something in the foreground it will be "on top." Begin with the waste-knot method (see page 18).

STEP 3 When the stitched line or shape is complete, take the needle through to the wrong side and run it through the backs of the stitches for about ¾ in. (2 cm) without piercing the fabric. Pull the needle through then snip the thread. Snip off the waste knot at the start and run in the tail in the same way. If the next line to be stitched touches the first, begin by running the needle through the backs of

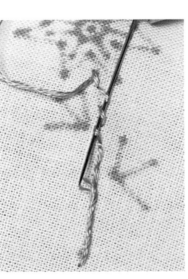

previous stitches. If the next line is any distance away, begin with another waste knot. Avoid passing the thread across the wrong side from one area to another; it is better to fasten off the thread and start again.

STEP 4 When the embroidery is complete, remove it from the hoop or frame. Traces of water-soluble pen may be removed by misting with water and leaving to dry. Press the work.

RABBIT CUSHION

Stitch this sweet cushion as a gift for a new baby, or as decoration for a small child's room.

Only five easy embroidery stitches are used, and the simple patchwork construction with

overlapping back panels (no zippers or fastenings) is explained in full.

TEMPLATE TO COPY

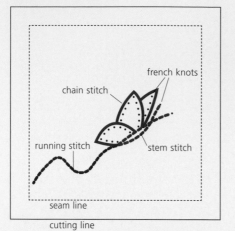

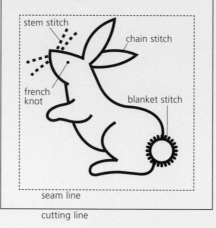

FINISHED SIZE 12 x 12 in. (30 x 30 cm)

MATERIALS
• Lightweight cotton or linen fabric in white: two squares each 8 x 8 in. (20 x 20 cm)
• Lightweight iron-on interfacing: two squares each 8 x 8 in. (20 x 20 cm)
• Embroidery hoop or frame
• Perle cotton No. 8: 8 yards (7 m) medium-blue, or substitute 4 yards (3.5 m) of stranded cotton embroidery floss and use three strands throughout
• Crewel needle, size 3
• Lightweight fabric in blue-and-white stripe: approximately 16 x 32 in. (40 x 81.5 cm)
• Sewing equipment: water-soluble marking pen, tape measure, scissors, pins, sharp sewing needle, white sewing thread, sewing machine (optional)
• Lightbox (optional)
• Masking tape
• Iron
• Cushion pad, 12 x 12 in. (30 x 30 cm)

TIPS
1. Choose another colorway for your cushion if you wish—any small-scale pattern can be substituted for the blue striped fabric used here—with the embroidery in any suitable color that is not too pale.
2. If your fabric has a regular, even stripe like ours, be sure to cut the pieces along straight lines of stripes.

ASSEMBLY INSTRUCTIONS

STEP 1
Photocopy the rabbit and butterfly outlines, enlarging by 300 percent. The outer squares (cutting lines) should measure 7¼ x 7¼ in. (18.5 x 18.5 cm).

STEP 2
Bond a square of interfacing to the wrong side of each square of white fabric, following the manufacturer's instructions. Overcast or machine zigzag all around each square with white sewing thread to prevent fraying.

STEP 3
Use a water-soluble fabric pen and the lightbox or window-pane method to trace the rabbit outline onto the right side of one square of white fabric, centering the outer square of the design on the fabric. Trace the butterfly outline onto the other white square in the same way. Don't trace the seam lines and cutting lines at this stage.

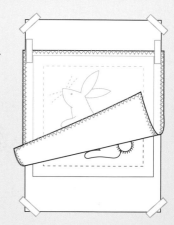

STEP 4

Mount each white square in turn in the embroidery frame or hoop and work the embroidery in the stitches indicated, following the Freestyle embroidery guidelines on page 59.

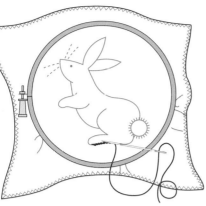

STEP 5
When the embroideries are complete, press each square face down on a well-padded surface. Return each square to the lightbox or window, matching the embroidery to the outline of the photocopy, and use the water-soluble fabric pen to trace the seam lines and cutting lines. Cut out the squares along the cutting lines. Make sure the seam lines are visible on the wrong side of each square: if not, place the square right side down on the lightbox and redraw the seam lines on the wrong side.

STEP 6
Use one embroidered square as a template to cut two matching squares of contrast lightweight fabric, here blue-and-white stripe. Also cut two rectangles, each 13¼ x 10½ in. (33.5 x 26.5 cm), from the contrast fabric.

STEP 7
Seam allowances throughout are ⅝ in. (1.5 cm). Place the rabbit square and one contrast square with right sides together and pin the seam to the left of the rabbit. Use white thread to backstitch or machine stitch along the marked seam line, then press the seam open on the wrong side. Join the butterfly square to the other contrast square in the same way, but join the seam to the right of the butterfly. Place the two pieces with right sides together, matching the previous seams, and join the center seam in the same way. Press this seam open.

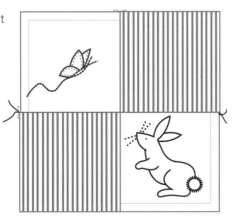

STEP 8
Turn a small double hem along one long edge of each contrast fabric rectangle and press. Machine stitch along the hems or hemstitch by hand. Place the two pieces right side up on a flat surface, overlapping as shown to form a square. Pin the overlapping edges in place.

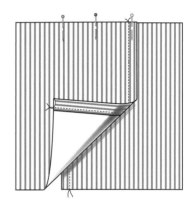

STEP 9
Pin the front panel right side down on top, then backstitch or machine stitch all around following the marked seam lines. Clip across the corners and turn right side out (see page 22). Mist with water to remove all traces of fabric pen, and press. Insert cushion pad.

SEE ALSO

Freestyle embroidery guidelines
   page 59
Lightbox tracing method page 58
Mounting in a hoop page 15
Blanket stitch page 106
Chain stitch page 108
Running stitch page 84
Stem stitch page 113
French knots page 116
Turning a hem page 23
Turning right side out page 22

TRANSFERRING DESIGNS

There are many products available to enable you to transfer designs onto fabric. Ready-printed iron-on transfers can be arranged on fabric in any way you wish. You can make your own transfers with a special pen or pencil, choosing any image you like. You can even print a photograph or drawing onto fabric, then stitch over it.

IRON-ON EMBROIDERY TRANSFERS

Iron-on embroidery transfers are printed on lightweight paper with special ink—usually blue or silver—that melts into the fabric when the back of the transfer is ironed.

STEP 1
Cut out the transfer with plenty of spare paper around it. Pin the transfer by the corners, ink side down, where required on the fabric. Heat the iron to a medium setting suitable for your fabric. The hottest part of the iron plate is at the center. Place the iron over the transfer area and leave for about 10 seconds. Do not move the iron around as this may blur the transferred lines. For large designs, lift and replace the iron until all areas have been treated. Avoid ironing over the pins.

NOTES
- A transfer image is printed in reverse, and is normally indelible.
- Most transfers print at a fairly low heat setting, so they are suitable for most fabrics, but fabrics with a smooth surface give the best results.
- If possible, test the iron setting and time required by using a spare piece of transfer and a small piece of your intended fabric, and always follow the manufacturer's instructions, if available.

STEP 2
Carefully lift one corner of the transfer to see if the design has transferred. If not, press again for a longer time, and/or increase the heat setting on the iron.

STEP 3
When the design has transferred successfully, remove the transfer paper and work your embroidery. The transfer ink is usually indelible, so the design lines must be covered by the stitching. Shaded satin stitch and French knots were used to stitch this flower.

DRAW YOUR OWN TRANSFER

Special transfer pens and pencils allow you to make your own transfers on tracing or greaseproof paper. You will also need an ordinary pencil.

NOTES

- Some transfers can be used two or three times before they fade. They can then be re-inked with a transfer pen and reused.
- It is a good idea to test the ironing process on spare fabric.

STEP 1 Use a pencil to trace your chosen design onto tracing paper.

STEP 2 Turn the tracing over and redraw all the lines with the special pen or pencil. Some transfer pens make rather heavy lines, so draw a series of dots instead.

STEP 3 ◁ Transfer the design according to the pen manufacturer's instructions, or in the same way as for the iron-on printed transfer, opposite page. The design will be the same way around as the original pencil tracing.

STEP 4 ◁ These transfers are usually indelible and must therefore be covered by the stitching. This lily was stitched with chain stitch, stem stitch, bullion knots, and single seeding.

SEE ALSO

Freestyle embroidery guidelines page 59
Satin stitch page 110
French knots page 116
Chain stitch page 108
Stem stitch page 113
Bullion knots page 118
Seeding stitch page 115
Shaded satin stitch page 112

PHOTO-TRANSFERS

PHOTO-TRANSFER METHODS

There are several products on the market intended for transferring photocopies or computer printouts onto T-shirts, which are great fun for the embroiderer to experiment with. Start with a favorite photograph, a drawing, or a computer-generated image, transfer it to fabric, and decorate it with embroidery in any way you like.

PHOTO-TRANSFER PASTE

The paste-on type of photo-transfer requires a photocopy of the original design. Follow the instructions supplied with the product. The photograph of poppies in a field was photocopied in color, then transferred to white cotton fabric, and highlighted with blanket stitch, stem stitch, seeding stitch, and French knots, using single strands of cotton embroidery floss. The embroidery is a reverse of the original photograph.

NOTES

- Choose white fabric so that printed colors will remain true.
- Wash, dry, and iron the fabric before commencing to remove any sizing.
- You can copy a small image several times onto one sheet of photo-transfer paper.
- Always make one or two test pieces to try out different thicknesses of photo-transfer paste, or heat settings and ironing times. You can cut away from the photocopy or the transfer print any parts of a picture you don't want and use them for testing. When preparing a drawing, you can draw a few squiggles in one corner to use for testing.
- Always test on exactly the same fabric as you intend to use. For a ready-made item, test on the inside of a hem.
- Always follow the instructions supplied with the product.
- Most photo-transfers leave a film across the surface of the fabric. As you stitch, the needle makes visible holes in this film. So use the finest needle you can, and try not to unpick any stitches.
- You can also use photo-transfer paste or paper to transfer an image onto white canvas, then embroider it in half cross-stitch.

△ ORIGINAL PHOTOGRAPH

▷ STITCHED SAMPLE

PHOTO-TRANSFER PAPER

There are several types of heat-transfer photo-paper available, suitable for different types of printers. Make sure you buy the right type for the printer you want to use. The image is photocopied onto the special paper, or printed from a computer, then transferred to the fabric by heating with an iron, as instructed by the manufacturer. Quite a lot of heat is usually necessary, so this method is not recommended for fabrics that will only withstand cool ironing.

SEE ALSO
Freestyle embroidery guidelines
    page 59
Cross-stitch guidelines page 26
French knots page 116
Stem stitch page 113
Blanket stitch page 106
Seeding stitch page 115
Cross-stitch page 86
Double running stitch page 82

STEP 1 This drawing by Amy Blank (age 7) was scanned into a computer, mirror-imaged, then printed out onto T-shirt transfer paper. Note the colored lines in the corner, to use for a test piece.

STEP 2 The design was transferred to Aida fabric, and is shown being worked in cross-stitch, double running stitch, and French knots.

PROJECT 10 FRAMED PORTRAIT

Turn a favorite photograph into a family heirloom. Using only simple embroidery stitches, this mounted and framed portrait makes a perfect gift.

FINISHED SIZE 10 x 8 in. (25 x 20 cm), or any size you choose

MATERIALS

• Picture frame with glass and backing board
• Cardboard window mount to fit frame
• Medium-weight smooth cotton fabric in white: at least 1 in. (2.5 cm) larger all around than the picture frame
• Photocopy or computer print-out of your chosen photograph
• Photo-transfer medium
• Embroidery hoop or frame
• Stranded cotton, silk, or rayon embroidery floss: approximately 5 yards (4.5 m) in each of five colors, all of similar intensity
• Crewel needle, size 7
• Large, sharp needle
• Strong thread, such as perle cotton size 8
• Sewing equipment: water-soluble fabric pen, scissors, sharp sewing needle, white sewing thread, sewing machine (optional)
• Iron

EMBROIDERY NOTES

Buy the frame and window mount before planning the embroidery. A window mount will keep the embroidery from touching the glass. Enlarge or reduce the photograph by photocopying, to suit the size of the window.
Carefully follow the instructions supplied with the transfer medium. You may need to photocopy or print out your image onto plain paper, or onto the special paper supplied.
If you use a computer-printed image, you may be able to make a mirror image, so the final portrait is not reversed.
We chose five pastel shades of thread to suit our faded sepia photograph. For a color photograph, you might choose brighter shades, but they should be of a similar intensity to prevent the background from looking spotty.
Follow the Freestyle embroidery guidelines on page 59. Use the size 7 needle and two strands of embroidery floss, or an equivalent thickness of other thread, for all the embroidery, following the instructions in Step 3.

ASSEMBLY INSTRUCTIONS

STEP 1 Wash, dry, and iron the cotton fabric. Overcast or machine zigzag all around the raw edges with white sewing thread. Center the window mount over the flat fabric and use a water-soluble fabric pen to draw lightly around the window to indicate the embroidery area. Cut away any unwanted areas from the transfer image and apply the transfer to the fabric, following the manufacturer's instructions and placing it as desired within the marked area.

STEP 2 Use the fabric pen to draw small circles and ovals, approximately ⅜ in. (1 cm) in diameter, scattered evenly across the background—you can use a circular stencil if you prefer. Put a dot in the center of each circle. Mark some partial circles around the edge of the image. Overlap the marked outer lines. Then fill the gaps between the circles with smaller circles, approximately ¼ in. (6 mm) in diameter, and scattered dots.

STEP 3
Mount the fabric in an embroidery hoop or frame, which should be large enough to take the whole embroidery area at once. With the first color of embroidery thread, stitch about one-third of the larger circles and ovals with six single chain stitches to make daisies. With the second color, stitch another third of these circles with eight blanket stitches, spikes pointing outward. With the third color, stitch the remaining third of these circles with six fly stitches, their tails meeting at the center to form little stars. With the fourth color, stitch all the small circles as six to eight blanket stitches with their spikes meeting at the center. With the fifth color, work all the dots as small French knots and add a dot at the center of each daisy.

STEP 4
When the embroidery is complete, do not press, as this may damage the transfer image. Mist with water and leave stretched in the hoop or frame to dry completely.

STEP 5
Remove the hoop or frame. Lay the embroidery right side down on a flat surface with the backing board at the center. Fold two opposite sides of the fabric over the board. Thread the large, sharp needle from the spool of strong thread, without cutting the thread. Lace the two edges together as shown, pulling extra thread from the spool as required. Fasten off with a backstitch and cut leaving a 4 in. (10 cm) end, then tighten the thread back toward the spool. Cut it and fasten off in the same way.

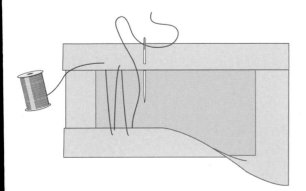

STEP 6
Fold in the remaining two edges and lace them in a similar way, without fastening off. Turn the work over and check with the window mount that the position is correct. At this stage you can adjust the lacing if necessary. When the placement is correct, fasten off all the ends securely with two or three backstitches.

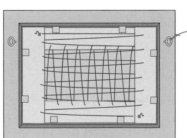

STEP 7
Place the frame right side down on a flat surface. Clean the inside of the glass and put it in the frame, then the window mount, then the mounted embroidery. If the frame is deep enough, you can add a layer of cardboard to cover the lacing. Fold down the tabs to hold the back in place. You may need to add a picture plate, or eyelets and string (or picture wire) for hanging.

SEE ALSO

Freestye embroidery
  guidelines page 59
Mounting in a hoop page 15
Photo-transfer page 64
Backstitch page 80

Blanket stitch page 106
Fly stitch page 114
Single chain stitch page 109
French knots page 116

CHOOSING AND USING STABILIZERS

Use a stabilizer when stitching delicate fabric, or working on a densely stitched area, to prevent puckering and distortion. Embroidery stabilizers are available in many forms: they may be non-woven fabric or paper, iron-on, self-adhesive, or soluble in water. Choosing the right stabilizer for your fabric and project will help you obtain the results you want. If possible, make a test piece using scraps of your fabric and stabilizer.

IRON-ON (FUSIBLE) INTERFACING

This product can be used to permanently strengthen lightweight and delicate fabrics for embroidery, and to prevent fraying. It is normally sold for dressmaking and is available in a variety of weights, from ultralight to heavyweight. A lightweight grade is fine for most projects.

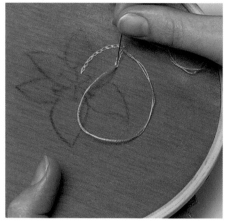

STEP 1 Transfer the design to the right side of the fabric, or trace it with a non-soluble marker such as a quilter's chalk pencil.

STEP 2 Cut the interlining to the same size as the fabric and bond it to the wrong side, following the manufacturer's instructions. If this involves steaming through a damp cloth, leave the fabric flat to dry completely.

STEP 3 For extra security, baste or machine zigzag all around the edge before mounting the fabric in a hoop or frame. Work the embroidery through both layers.

STEP 4 The finished embroidery will be quite stable.

NOTES

- Choose an iron-on interfacing to suit your fabric: some grades require only a medium iron, making them suitable for silks and other delicate fabrics; others require more heat, so use these for fabrics such as cotton and linen.
- Back the whole piece of fabric, not just the area to be embroidered.
- Many iron-on interfacings are bonded to the fabric by pressing through a damp cloth. Test this process beforehand with spare scraps to make sure the steam does not spoil your fabric.
- Don't use a water-soluble pen to trace designs, as ironing with steam will remove the tracing.

SELF-ADHESIVE STABILIZER

This type of stabilizer usually consists of a non-woven fabric with a sticky back, mounted on a peel-off paper backing. It is used as a temporary stabilizer during stitching, then removed when the work is complete.

STEP 1 Trace or transfer the design to the right side of the fabric.

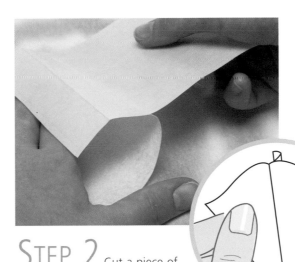

STEP 2 Cut a piece of stabilizer at least 1 in. (2.5 cm) larger all around than the design area. Peel off the backing paper and smooth the sticky side of the stabilizer onto the wrong side of the fabric.

STEP 3 Mount the fabric in a hoop or frame and work the embroidery through both layers. Fasten off the thread ends securely, dab them with anti-fray solution, and allow to dry.

STEP 4 Working on a hard surface, use the point of a darning needle to lightly score through the stabilizer, all around the embroidery, as close to the stitching as possible.

STEP 5 Gently pull away the excess pieces of stabilizer. Tweezers are useful for small scraps. Tiny shreds may be left in place. Large pieces of stabilizer can be replaced on the backing paper and kept to use again.

WATER-SOLUBLE STABILIZERS

Various thicknesses of water-soluble paper and non-woven fabric stabilizers are available. The paper type is particularly useful because it can also carry the design outline.

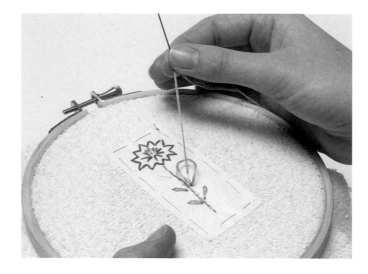

STEP 1 Trace, transfer, or print
the design onto the water-soluble paper. Cut the paper at least ½ in. (12 mm) outside the design, and pin it in place on the fabric. Baste the paper in position, then work the embroidery through both layers together. It is not really necessary to use a hoop or frame if the paper is sufficiently stiff, but use one if you wish.

STEP 2 When
the embroidery is complete, gently pull out the basting and tear away large areas of excess paper.

NOTES
- Use this type of stabilizer for embroidery on fabrics that are too heavy for the design to be traced, or too heavily textured for the design to be transferred.
- Stretch fabrics, such as fleece or stretch velvet, should also be backed with self-adhesive stabilizer, as on the previous page.
- Use this technique for embroidery on ready-made items that are difficult to mount in a hoop or frame.
- Fabrics must be washable.
- Designs may be traced onto water-soluble paper using a dry medium such as a quilter's chalk pencil, heat-transferred, or printed from a computer using a light gray tone (dark lines may bleed into the fabric).

STEP 3 Dissolve the
paper following the manufacturer's instructions. Some fabrics, such as silks, may be susceptible to water staining and the whole piece must be gently washed. Lay flat to dry.

STEP 4

If a fluffy residue remains around the stitches, or the fabric feels stiff, then the stabilizer has not completely dissolved and Step 3 should be repeated. Allow the work to dry flat, then press.

SEE ALSO

Tracing designs page 58
Transferring designs page 62
Mounting in a hoop or frame
   page 15
Freestyle embroidery guidelines
   page 59
Pressing page 20

STITCHING ON READY-MADES

All kinds of ready-made articles can be decorated with embroidery, such as shirts, T-shirts, jeans, bed linen, table linen, and baby clothes. The area you wish to decorate may be perfectly accessible, but difficult to hold in a hoop or frame, so the right choice of stabilizer will help you achieve a neat result.

The collar of this shirt is easily embroidered without a hoop, using water-soluble paper to carry the design. The flower motif is taken from page 58.

This jersey baby hat is stretchy, so the motif area was backed with self-adhesive stabilizer. The butterfly from page 60 was reduced, traced onto water-soluble paper, and embroidered.

PROJECT 11 FLOWERY T-SHIRT

Dress up a plain T-shirt with your own original embroidery: stitch all three flowers, or just one for a child-size top. T-shirt fabric is stretchy, so self-adhesive embroidery stabilizer is a must.

TEMPLATE TO COPY

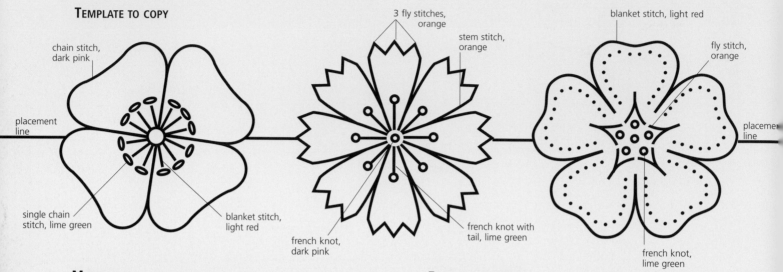

chain stitch, dark pink

3 fly stitches, orange

stem stitch, orange

blanket stitch, light red

fly stitch, orange

placement line

placement line

single chain stitch, lime green

blanket stitch, light red

french knot, dark pink

french knot with tail, lime green

french knot, lime green

MATERIALS

- Plain cotton T-shirt or top
- Self-adhesive embroidery stabilizer, 1 in. (2.5 cm) larger than the embroidery hoop
- Embroidery hoop: for three flowers, at least 8 in. (20 cm) in diameter
- Stranded cotton embroidery floss: for three flowers, 1½ yards (1.1 m) light red, 1½ yards (1.1 m) orange, 1 yard (0.9 m) dark pink, 1 yard (0.9 m) lime green; for one flower, your choice of colors
- Tapestry needle, size 26
- Sewing equipment: water-soluble fabric pen, tape measure, scissors
- Lightbox (optional)
- Masking tape
- White bar soap
- Anti-fray solution
- Tweezers

EMBROIDERY NOTES

Follow the Freestyle embroidery guidelines on page 59. Use two strands of stranded embroidery floss for all the embroidery. Use a small tapestry needle; a sharp needle will tend to split the threads of the T-shirt fabric, making it difficult to pull through the surface.

ASSEMBLY INSTRUCTIONS

STEP 1 Photocopy the flower outline.

STEP 2 Decide where you want to position the motifs on the T-shirt. For our example, we placed a ruler straight across the front, 1½ in. (4 cm) above the level of the armholes, and used a water-soluble fabric pen to draw a line 8 in. (20 cm) long, marking the center point.

TIPS

1. Do not press hard when tracing on stretchy fabric; you can trace each line as a series of dots to avoid distortion.
2. Try on the T-shirt to make sure you are happy with the tracing placement. At this stage, you can erase the design by misting it with water, then allow the shirt to dry, press it, and start again.
3. Large pieces of stabilizer can be saved to use again by smoothing them back onto the backing paper.

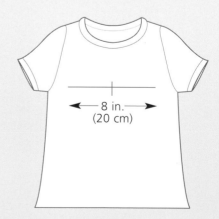

8 in. (20 cm)

STEP 3 Tape the photocopy to a lightbox or a sunny window pane. Position the T-shirt on top of the photocopy and match the line on the shirt to the placement line, and the center mark to the center of the middle flower. A small lightbox may be slipped inside the T-shirt if the light is not bright enough to show the design through both layers. Hold or tape the shirt in place and use the water-soluble fabric pen to trace the lines of the design.

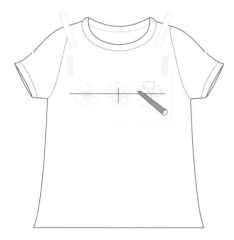

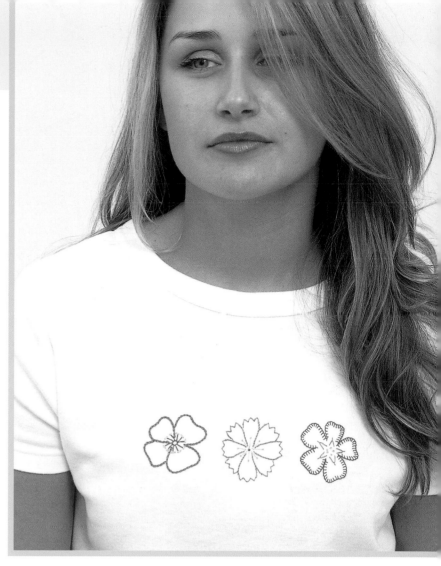

STEP 4 Turn the T-shirt inside out. Peel off the backing paper from the self-adhesive stabilizer and smooth it firmly on the wrong side of the design. To avoid a sticky residue building up on the needle as you stitch, rub a little white bar soap on the stabilizer behind each motif.

STEP 6 Turn the T-shirt inside out and place it on a firm, flat surface. Use a sharp pin or needle to lightly score around the outline of each motif, just outside the stitching. Then gently tear away as much stabilizer as possible (see page 69). Remove any traces of water-soluble pen by misting with water. Press on the wrong side, protecting the back of the embroidery with a dry cloth.

STEP 5 Turn the T-shirt right side out and slip the inside ring of an embroidery hoop inside the shirt, then mount the area in the hoop. Follow the embroidery guidelines to stitch the flowers. Make sure all the ends are run in securely along the backs of the stitches. When the embroidery is complete, remove the hoop, then dab each thread end with a tiny dot of anti-fray solution and allow to dry.

SEE ALSO
Freestyle embroidery guidelines
    page 59
Lightbox tracing method page 58
Mounting in a hoop page 15
Self-adhesive stabilizer page 69
Blanket stitch page 106
Chain stitch page 108
Single chain stitch page 109
Stem stitch page 113
French knots page 116
French knot with tail page 117
Fly stitch page 114

SIMPLE APPLIQUÉ

For bright, bold effects try the simple technique of appliqué. Shapes are cut from contrasting fabrics and bonded in place with fusible web, then decorated with embroidery.

For a motif 6 x 4 in. (15 x 10 cm), enlarge this design by 200% by photocopying.

STEP 1
Use a lightbox and a water-soluble fabric pen to trace the outline of the design onto the background fabric. (For heavy fabrics you can prepare your own transfer, or simply place the appliqué pieces by eye at Step 6.) Trace the design in pencil onto tracing paper. Turn the tracing over and redraw the lines with a black fiber-tip pen. The design is now in reverse.

STEP 2
Lay fusible web over the reversed design, paper side up, and trace the appliqué shapes with pencil. Position the shapes to make economical use of the fusible web, but leave at least ½ in. (12 mm) between them.

STEP 3
Cut out the shapes, leaving about ¼ in. (6 mm) all around each one.

NOTES
- The raw edge of each appliqué piece is usually covered with embroidery, such as blanket stitch, to prevent fraying.
- Applying fusible web involves steaming with a hot iron, so smooth cotton or linen fabrics are the most suitable.
- On patterned backgrounds, the appliqué fabrics must be sufficiently heavy for the pattern not to show through.
- For stitching on lightweight fabrics, two or three strands of cotton embroidery floss, or equivalent, are suitable. For heavier fabrics, use more strands or a heavier thread.

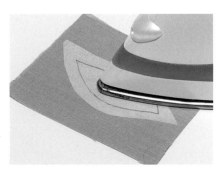

STEP 4
Following the manufacturer's instructions, iron the cutouts to the wrong side of your appliqué fabrics.

STEP 5
Now cut out each fabric shape accurately.

SEE ALSO
Tracing designs page 58
Freestyle embroidery guidelines page 59
Blanket stitch page 106
Stem stitch page 113
French knots with tails page 117
Beads and sequins page 52

STEP 6
Peel off the backing paper from each piece in turn and bond it in place on the background fabric, following the manufacturer's instructions.

STEP 7
Use the water-soluble fabric pen to mark guidelines for the embroidery. Lines that are worked on the background fabric may be re-traced from the design if they have disappeared during bonding. Work blanket stitch, or a similar stitch, all around each appliqué piece, using thread to complement the appliqué fabric. We used closed blanket stitch for the leaf: pairs of blanket stitches are worked into the same hole, forming a row of triangles.

MOTIFS FROM PRINTED FABRICS
You can also apply motifs cut from printed fabrics. Back the area of your chosen motif with fusible web, cut it out, and complete as Steps 6–8 as above.

STEP 8
Other stitches suitable for edging appliqué motifs include: couching, herringbone stitch, and cross-stitch. We worked the stem and leaf vein in stem stitch and the flower center in French knots with tails, adding a bead at the center. When the embroidery is complete, remove it from the hoop or frame and mist it with water to remove all traces of water-soluble pen. Press the work.

CHEF'S APRON

Use fusible web appliqué to add bright, bold motifs to the pocket of this simple apron, an ideal gift for any cook (or gardener).

MATERIALS
- Dressmakers' pattern paper with 2 in. (5 cm) squares, 14 x 40 in. (70 x 100 cm)
- Pencil
- Medium-weight cotton fabric in blue-and-cream stripe, approximately 28 x 40 in (70 x 100 cm)
- Scraps of medium-weight cotton fabric: light red, dark red, and bright green
- Fusible web, 10 x 10 in. (25 x 25 cm)
- Stranded cotton embroidery floss: approximately 2 yards (1.9 m) each of light red, dark red, and bright green, to match scrap fabrics
- Crewel needle, size 7
- Bias binding in cream, 1 yard (91.5 cm)
- Woven cotton tape in cream, 2½ yards (2.3 m)
- Sewing equipment: water-soluble fabric pen, tape measure, scissors, pins, sharp sewing needle, cream sewing thread, sewing machine
- Iron

EMBROIDERY NOTES
Follow the Freestyle embroidery guidelines on page 59. Use two strands of embroidery floss for all the embroidery.

TEMPLATE TO COPY

TIP
Wash, dry, and iron all fabrics before commencing, to prevent uneven shrinkage in the future.

ASSEMBLY INSTRUCTIONS

STEP 1
Enlarge the apron and pocket patterns by copying them onto dressmakers' pattern paper. Each square on the pattern diagrams represents one 2 in. (5 cm) square on the paper. Cut out the full-size paper patterns. On the apron pattern, pierce two small holes at the black dots. Enlarge the vegetable appliqué designs, above right, by 200 percent on a photocopier.

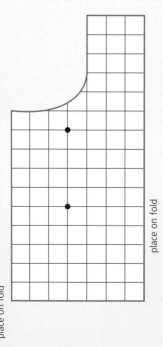

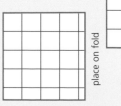

place on fold

place on fold

STEP 2
Fold the blue-and-cream striped fabric in half, matching the long edges. Make sure the fold lies along the straight grain of the fabric, at the center of a stripe. Pin the pattern pieces to the fabric, matching the edges to the fold as shown. Use lots of pins, pointing out from the center. Cut out the apron and pocket through both thicknesses of fabric. On the apron, use a water-soluble fabric pen to mark the fabric through the two pierced holes. At each hole, push a pin straight through to mark the other side in the corresponding position. Unpin the paper patterns.

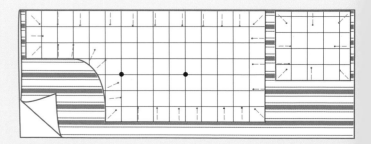

STEP 3
Fold the pocket piece in half, matching the two short edges, and press the fold to mark the center. Then fold and press ½ in. (12 mm) to wrong side along both short edges and one long edge. On remaining long edge, fold and press ¼ in. (6 mm) to wrong side, then fold again by a further ¾ in. (18 mm) and press again. This edge will be the top of the pocket. Unfold all the edges.

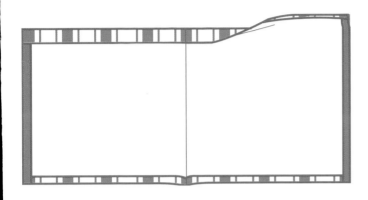

STEP 4
Work the appliqué following Appliqué guidelines on pages 74–75, arranging the motifs by eye within the folded hem lines.

complete tomato outline here | complete pepper outline here | blanket stitch

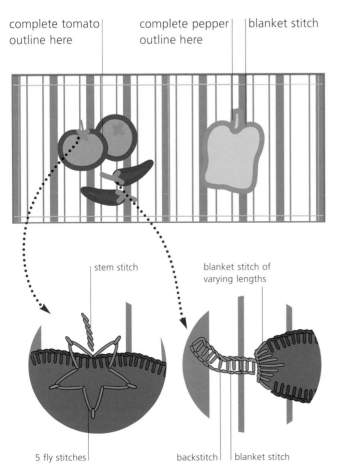

stem stitch

blanket stitch of varying lengths

5 fly stitches | backstitch | blanket stitch

STEP 5
Refold the top edge of the pocket as before and pin in place. Machine stitch with matching thread close to the fold. Fold under the remaining three sides as before, then pin in place on the apron, matching the corners to the marked dots. Machine stitch around three sides, beginning and ending with a neat triangle at each top corner as shown, to make the seam really strong. Sew up the center fold line, ending with a triangle at the top.

STEP 6
Bind the curved edges with bias binding as on page 23. Turn a small hem along each side edge, and matching hems at top and bottom edges, as on page 23. For the neck loop, cut 24 in. (60 cm) of cream cotton tape. Pin one end under each top corner of the apron, overlapping by about 1 in. (2.5 cm), then stitch firmly in a square as shown. Cut the remaining tape in half and stitch one end of each piece to each waist corner in the same way. At the free end of each waist tie, fold and stitch a small double hem.

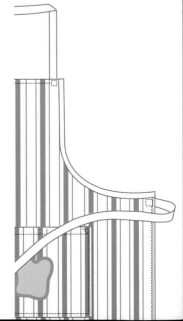

stitch
library

In this section, step-by-step photographs and text show you how to work all of the stitches used in this book. Some stitches are mainly used for counted thread embroidery and some for freestyle, while others may be used for both types of work. The Sampler File below each stitch description illustrates the various applications of each stitch.

BACKSTITCH

Backstitch forms a firm, solid line, often used as an outline for cross-stitch or blackwork. The same stitch is also used to make firm seams (see page 21).

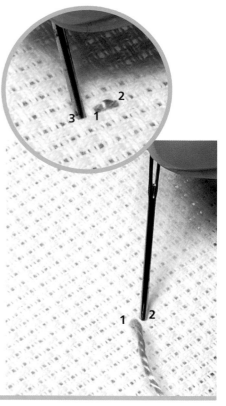

STEP 1 Begin with the waste-knot method (see page 18). Working from right to left, bring the needle up at 1, a short distance—on Aida fabric one or more squares—along the required line.

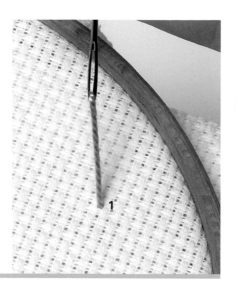

STEP 2 Insert the needle back at the beginning of the line, at 2. Pull through to the back of the work. Bring the needle up again, further along the line at 3.

STEP 3 Insert the needle at 1, the end of the previous stitch, and pull through to the back. Repeat as required, making all the stitches the same length.

Backstitches may be worked as straight lines or stepped to form zigzags and curves. A line of backstitch may then be whipped or laced.

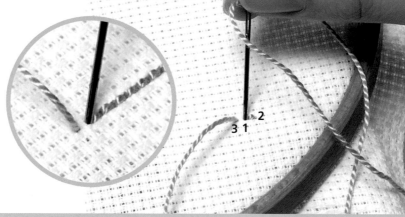

WHIPPED BACKSTITCH

Whipping a line of backstitch adds emphasis to an outline and also smoothes out the steps of a curve. The whipping may be in a contrast color for a decorative effect, or you can use the same color to make an existing backstitch line bolder.

STEP 1
Begin with the waste-knot method (see page 18). Using the same or a contrasting thread, bring the needle up at 1, the center of the first backstitch, below the thread.

STEP 2
Pass the needle under the next stitch from top to bottom, from 2 to 3, without piercing the fabric or the backstitch. Repeat along the whole line, without pulling the thread too tightly. At the end of the line, pass the needle through the fabric underneath the center of the last backstitch. Fasten off thread ends by running them in along the wrong side of the backstitches.

LACED BACKSTITCH
Various decorative effects may be achieved by lacing a line of backstitch.

Begin as Step 1 of Whipped Backstitch (above), then pass the needle alternately up and down beneath the backstitches, from 2 to 3 then from 4 to 5. Do not pull the lacing thread too tightly. Finish the thread ends in the same way as for whipped backstitch.

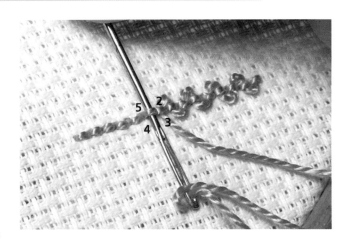

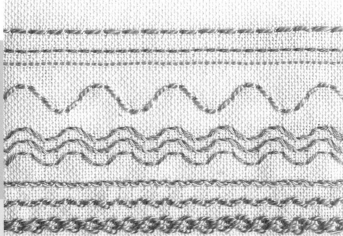

Backstitch, whipped backstitch, and laced backstitch worked on evenweave fabric. The lowest line shows two lines of backstitch laced together, with a second lacing thread added to make a chain effect.

DOUBLE RUNNING STITCH

This stitch is often used for outlines and for blackwork patterns. It looks identical to backstitch on the front of the work, but is much neater on the back and less bulky.

STEP 1 Begin with the waste-knot method (see page 18). For a straight line, work from right to left. On Aida fabric stitches may sometimes be several squares in length—two squares here. Bring the needle up at 1, down at 2, up at 3, down at 4, and so on along a straight row of holes as for running stitch (see page 84).

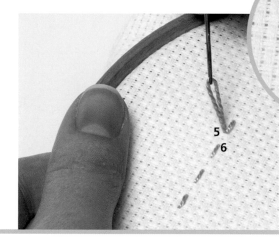

STEP 2 At the end of the line, turn the work and stitch back along the line, filling each gap with another stitch. To make a straight line, bring the needle up above the thread of the existing stitch at 5, and insert the needle below the thread of the next stitch at 6. All the stitches will then slope very slightly in the same direction, making a smooth, even line.

STEP 3 On the wrong side of the work, the stitches follow the design line exactly. Run the thread ends along the backs of the stitches to fasten them off.

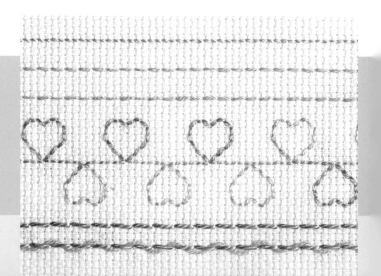

Double running stitch on Aida fabric. The lowest line has been laced in the same way as laced backstitch (see pages 80–81).

LINES WITH SPRIGS

Decorative borders often include lines with "sprigs," formed using double running stitch.

STEP 1 Work along the line
in running stitch (see page 84) from right to left. At each sprig, work out to the end of the sprig and back again to the line as for double running stitch (page 82), so each sprig is complete.

STEP 2 At the end of the
line, turn the work and stitch back again, completing the line.

On evenweave fabric, stitches may be two or more threads (or intersections) in length. On the line of squares, alternate squares have been whipped in the same way as whipped backstitch (see pages 80–81); notice how this whipping rounds off the corners.

RUNNING STITCH

Sometimes called darning stitch, this simple stitch is very easy to work on Aida fabric or evenweave. Decorative patterns can be made with simple blocks of color, or zigzag arrangements, and the stitches may be whipped or laced in the same way as for backstitch (see pages 80–81).

Lines may be worked from left to right or vice versa. Begin with the waste-knot method (see page 18). Take the needle up at 1 and down at 2 through the fabric along a straight row of holes at the required intervals. Fasten off by running the thread ends along the backs of the stitches.

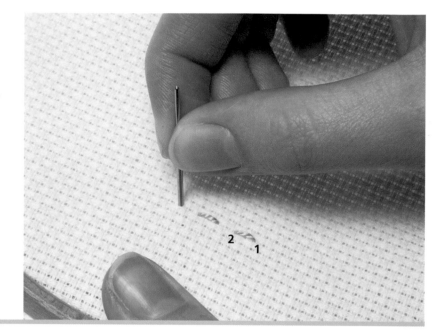

Running stitches worked on Aida fabric. The third line from the top is whipped, and the fourth line is laced (see pages 80–81). Patterns may be formed in zigzags or blocks of stitches. At the bottom, four lines of running stitch are laced together.

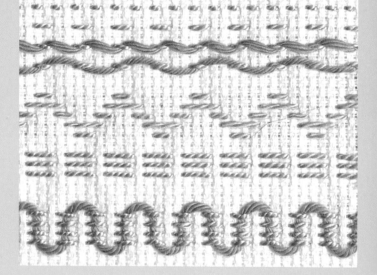

Running stitches on evenweave can be worked with just one fabric thread between the lines, making more solid patterns. At the bottom, ten lines of running stitch are laced in pairs to form an all-over wave pattern.

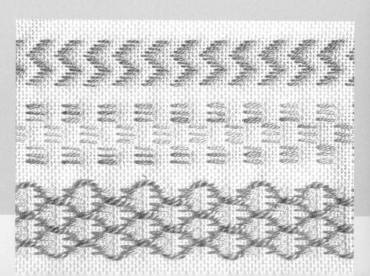

HALF CROSS-STITCH

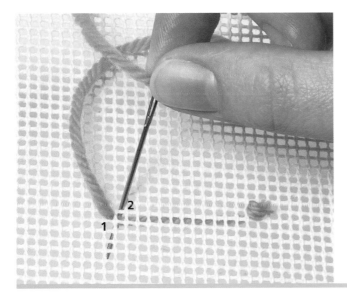

This stitch is most often worked on canvas, when the thread should be thick enough for the stitches to completely hide the canvas mesh (see page 42). It may be worked from a chart (see page 30), or designs may be printed, or drawn by hand, onto the canvas. It may also be used as part of a cross-stitch design.

STEP 1 To fill an area, begin at top left using the stitch-to-the-knot method (see page 18). Bring the needle up at 1, the lower left corner of the canvas intersection—or fabric square—to be covered, and take it down at 2, the opposite corner, making a slanting stitch from bottom left to top right. Repeat to the right.

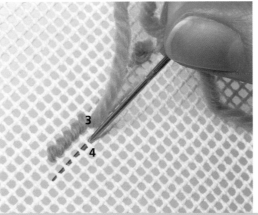

STEP 2 Work the next line, below the first, from right to left, bringing the needle up at 3, top right, and taking it down at 4, bottom left. On this line you bring the needle up through a hole that already contains a thread. Repeat these two lines downward to fill the area.

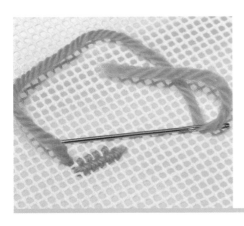

STEP 3 On the wrong side, the stitches form a series of vertical lines. Run the thread ends in along the backs of the stitches.

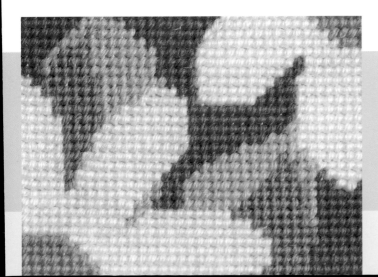

Half-cross stitch worked on canvas. The outline of this design was traced onto the canvas using colored pencils. Beginning with the foreground—the petals—each area was stitched in the appropriate color, interpreting the outlines to make smooth curves. The background color was stitched last.

CROSS-STITCH

Basic cross-stitch may be worked as single crosses, or stitched in lines to fill areas with color. It is most often stitched on Aida fabric, using the pattern of squares to keep the crosses uniform in size. Cross-stitch on evenweave fabric is almost as easy, working each stitch over two (or more) threads in each direction. Using a tapestry needle with a blunt point it is easy to find the holes in either fabric and so avoid splitting fabric threads.

CROSS-STITCH WORKED SINGLY
By this method, each cross-stitch is completed before moving on to the next.

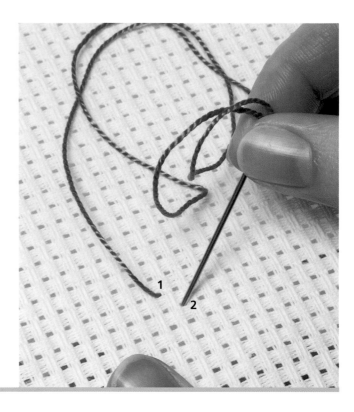

STEP 1 If you are filling a solid shape with cross-stitch, begin at bottom left of the area, using the stitch-to-the-knot method (see page 18). Bring the needle up at 1, the top left corner of the fabric square to be covered by the stitch, and take it down again at 2, the opposite corner. Pull through.

STEP 2 Bring the needle up again at 3, top right of the fabric square. Take the needle down at 4, the opposite corner. Note that the top thread of the cross slopes from top right to bottom left.

Cross-stitch on Aida fabric. This traditional cross-stitch border design does not contain large areas of continuous color, so the cross-stitches are worked singly, completing each cross before moving on to the next.

OPPOSITE: Cross-stitch on evenweave fabric. Each cross is worked over two fabric threads in each direction.

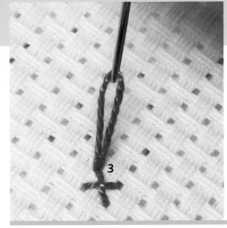

STEP 3 Bring the needle up at 3, the top right of the completed cross, to begin the next stitch to the right.

STEP 4 The next line of stitches is worked above the first line, in the same way but from right to left. Repeat these two lines upward as required.

CROSS-STITCH WORKED IN LINES

This method is a speedy way to fill large areas. The appearance is slightly different to cross-stitch worked singly, because the fabric is compressed in a different way—especially noticeable on a soft evenweave fabric—so avoid combining the two methods in the same area of color.

STEP 1 To fill an area, begin at top right using the stitch-to-the-knot method (see page 18). Bring the needle up at 1, the bottom right corner of the first square, and down at 2, the opposite corner. Repeat to the end of the line, making a series of slanting stitches.

STEP 2 Work back along the line from left to right, completing each cross in turn with a stitch from 3 to 4. Repeat these two lines downward.

TIPS

Plan your stitching so that you bring the needle up through an empty hole and take it down through a hole already occupied: this helps avoid splitting the embroidery floss.

All the top threads of the crosses should slope in the same direction—usually from top right to bottom left—otherwise the surface of the work will look uneven.

Cross-stitch designs are usually worked from a chart, as explained on page 30.

PART CROSS-STITCHES

Three-quarter cross-stitch is used along the curved or slanting edges of a cross-stitch shape, to soften the stepped effect formed by plain cross-stitch. Where two areas of color meet, three-quarter cross-stitches are worked in one color and quarter crosses in the other. These stitches may be represented on charts in several ways, so read your chart key carefully. Sometimes you have to decide for yourself which color is the three-quarter stitch and which the quarter: use the three-quarter stitch for the foreground object or area and the quarter stitch for the background.

THREE-QUARTER CROSS-STITCH
There are four different positions for a three-quarter cross-stitch within a fabric square. Either the lower or the upper thread will end at the center of the square.

STEP 1
Whichever corner of a fabric square you are filling, work the lower thread first, whether it is a full diagonal or just a half. For a half diagonal it is easier to bring the needle up at 1, the corner of the square, and insert it at 2, the center. Use the needle tip to carefully push the fabric threads apart at the center of the square.

Three-quarter cross-stitch on Aida fabric, smoothing the steps of curved and diagonal lines and edges.

OPPOSITE: On evenweave fabric, cross-stitch is normally worked over two fabric threads in each direction. So three-quarter and quarter crosses are easy to work because there is an easily found hole at the center of the square.

STEP 2 Complete the cross with a stitch from 3 to 4, so the top thread slopes in the same direction as the rest of the cross-stitches.

STEP 3 At this corner the lower thread, 5 to 6, is the full diagonal, worked first. The top thread is the half diagonal: bring the needle up at 7, the corner of the square, then push the fabric threads apart at the center (8) with the needle tip and insert the needle. The top thread will then cross over the lower thread.

QUARTER CROSS-STITCH
Bring the needle up at 1, the corner of the square, and insert it at 2, the center, through the same hole as the half diagonal of the adjacent three-quarter cross.

TIP
Where part cross-stitches edge an area of cross-stitch, work them at the same time as the full crosses to maintain an even appearance.

UPRIGHT CROSS-STITCH

This stitch is often used in blackwork and can be scattered, arranged in patterns, or worked closely together to fill an area.

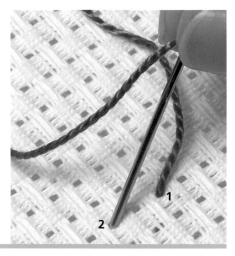

STEP 1
Begin with the waste-knot method (see page 18). Working from right to left, make a straight stitch from 1 to 2 across an even number of Aida squares, or evenweave threads. This stitch is two fabric squares in length.

STEP 2
Bring the needle up at the lower point of the cross (3) and insert it at the top (4) to make a vertical stitch.

STEP 3
To stitch a line of upright crosses, first make all the horizontal stitches, then work back along the line adding all the verticals.

Upright cross-stitches and star stitches (see page 91) may be worked singly or in lines, and arranged to form various patterns.

Star Stitch

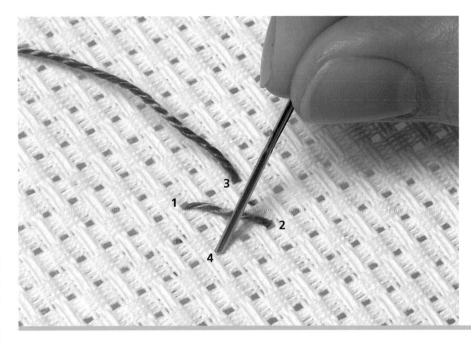

A basic cross-stitch (see page 86) and an upright cross-stitch (see page 90) join together to form the star stitch. Like the upright cross, the star stitch is often used in blackwork and may be scattered, arranged in patterns, or worked closely together to fill an area.

STEP 1
Begin by making a cross-stitch from 1 to 2, then 3 to 4, in the usual way, across two or more squares of an even number.

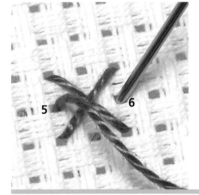

STEP 2
Make the horizontal stitch of an upright cross from 5 to 6.

STEP 3
Complete the star by adding the vertical stitch from 7 to 8.

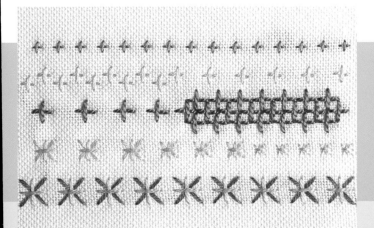

On evenweave fabric, upright cross-stitch and star stitch are always worked over an even number of threads in each direction.

FAN AND RAY STITCHES

Straight stitches on Aida fabric or canvas may be grouped into fans and rays, with several stitches sharing one hole at the base of the shape.

FANS ON FABRIC

On Aida fabric or evenweave, groups of three, four, or more straight stitches that share one hole at the base of each group are often called fans. The length and arrangement of the individual stitches may be varied to form a wide variety of patterns, but the way to work them all remains the same.

Begin with the stitch-to-the-knot method (see page 18). Bring the needle up at 1 on the outside edge of the fan, and insert it at the base, at 2. Bring the needle up at 3, 4, 5, and 6 in turn, always inserting at 2. Work the straight stitches of each group in the same order every time you repeat the group, to keep the appearance as regular as possible. The hole at 2 will be enlarged, and on some fabrics this effect is enhanced by pulling the stitches quite firmly.

Fans worked on Aida fabric in a variety of threads. Fans of three, four, or more stitches may be arranged as decorative lines or borders, or worked closely together to fill whole areas with pattern.

RAY STITCH ON CANVAS

Groups of three or more straight stitches that share one hole at the base are usually called ray stitches. The basic ray stitch is worked over a square block of canvas threads. Choose a thread thickness that will ensure the canvas is completely covered.

STEP 1 This ray stitch unit consists of seven stitches worked over a square of four holes in each direction. Begin at bottom left of the area with the stitch-to-the-knot method (see page 18). Always bring the needle up at the outer edge of the block and insert it at the shared hole.

STEP 2 Always work the stitches of each unit in the same order. Work a line of units from left to right. For the next line of units above, it is easier to fasten off the thread and begin again at the left, so that the needle always comes up through an empty hole.

DIAMOND RAY STITCH ON CANVAS

This is a ray stitch worked over a diamond shape instead of a square block of canvas. Choose a thread thickness that will ensure the canvas is completely covered.

Diamond ray stitch is worked in a similar way to ray stitch. The diamonds shown here consist of seven stitches each, although other sizes, with five, nine, or more stitches, are also possible. Begin at bottom left with the stitch-to-the-knot method (see page 18) and work the first line of units from left to right.

The next line of units above can be worked from right to left. If you also work the stitches of each unit from right to left, instead of left to right as on the first row, the appearance of the pattern will be slightly different.

At top left, each seven-stitch unit of ray stitch is worked over a square of four holes in each direction. Bottom left shows ray stitch in two colors, with each nine-stitch unit worked over a square of five holes. Top right shows diamond ray stitch in seven-stitch units, and at bottom right in nine-stitch units.

ALGERIAN EYE STITCH

Often used in blackwork, this stitch forms an eight-pointed star with an enlarged hole at the center.

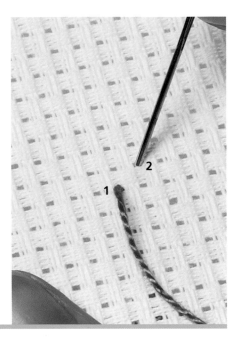

STEP 1
On Aida fabric an Algerian eye stitch is usually worked over a block of two, four, or six fabric squares in each direction, and on evenweave fabric over four, six, or more threads in each direction. Begin with the waste-knot method (see page 18). Bring the needle up at one corner of the block, at 1, and insert it at the center, at 2.

STEP 2
Working clockwise, bring the needle up at the middle of the next side of the block, at 3, and insert it again at 2, the central hole. Work clockwise around the block, always inserting the needle at the central hole.

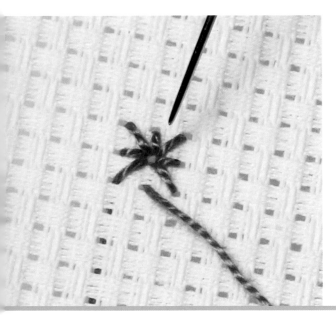

STEP 3
The central hole will be enlarged by the eight stitches passing through it.

When working Algerian eye stitches in a line, work each unit clockwise and in the same order. Top: Algerian eye stitches are shown worked over two and four Aida fabric squares. Bottom: large Algerian eyes worked over four and eight squares.

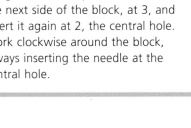

ENLARGED ALGERIAN EYE STITCH

A larger Algerian eye may be stitched over a block of four or eight Aida fabric squares by making sixteen stitches into the center—one at each corner and three along each side.

STEP 1 Work clockwise,
beginning at one corner (1). If necessary, enlarge the central hole (2) with the needle, pushing the threads farther apart. Work clockwise as with Algerian eye stitch (above), always inserting the needle at the central hole.

STEP 2 Here, the final
(sixteenth) stitch is being worked into the central hole.

Algerian eye stitch is often used for canvaswork, each unit covering a square of two or four threads in each direction. Sometimes the canvas threads show between the stitch units, when lines of backstitch (see page 80) in the same or a contrasting color may be added to cover them. The lowest line shows enlarged Algerian eye stitch worked over four threads in each direction.

HARDANGER STITCHES

Described on the following eight pages are the stitches most often used for Hardanger work. After working the Kloster blocks and withdrawing the threads, you can choose to work overcast bars or woven bars, or woven bars with picots. Then you can choose to fill some or all of the empty squares with loop-stitch filling, oblique-loop-stitch filling, or dove's-eye filling.

For further details on the technique of Hardanger work, see pages 48–49.

KLOSTER BLOCKS

A Kloster block is normally a group of five satin stitches worked over four threads of Hardanger fabric or evenweave. Count carefully to ensure accurate placing, so that when the threads are cut and withdrawn, the remaining threads are correctly secured. Choose the heavy thread and tapestry needle to suit your fabric from the table on page 48.

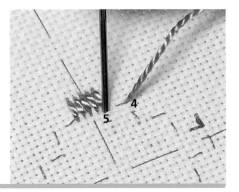

STEP 1 Baste the outline of the design onto the fabric (see page 50). Begin with the waste-knot method (see page 18). Work clockwise around a shape. Bring the needle up at 1, the outside left corner of a block. Count four threads in toward the inside of the design and insert the needle at 2. Bring the needle out again one thread to the right of 1, at 3.

STEP 2 Repeat the stitch four more times, making a block of five stitches, then bring the needle out again at the nearest outside corner of the next block (4) and insert it four threads toward the inside of the design, at 5.

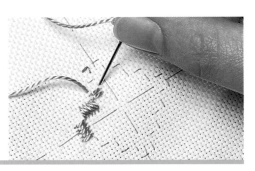

STEP 3 Continue working around the shape, following the chart carefully, until you return to the starting point.

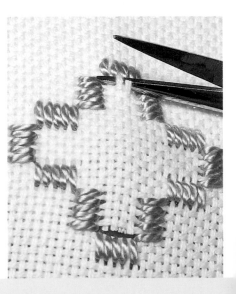

STEP 4 To finish a thread, run the end beneath three or more blocks on the wrong side and snip off the excess. Snip off the waste knot and run in the starting end in the same way. The threads may now be cut and withdrawn (see Steps 3–5, page 49), ready for bars and fillings to be worked.

Overcast bars

Sometimes called wrapped bars, these are worked on the grid of threads left after the cut threads are withdrawn. Use the finer thread and needle from the table on page 48. Plan the order of working the bars before you begin: the easiest way is usually to begin at a corner and work diagonally across the shape and back again.

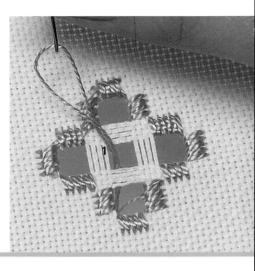

STEP 1 Secure the thread on the wrong side of the work by slipping it under three or four Kloster blocks, and bring it out at 1, through the empty square, at lower left of the first group of threads to be overcast.

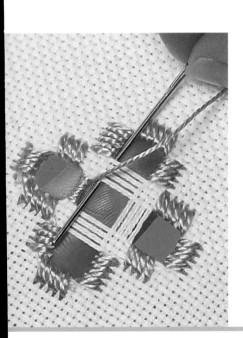

STEP 2 Take the needle around the bar several times, wrapping it tightly. The threads should lie neatly side by side without overlapping. Count the wraps you make to cover the bar, and make all the bars the same.

STEP 3 At the end of the bar, move diagonally on to the next bar and overcast it in exactly the same way— you may need to slip the needle through the backs of the Kloster blocks to reach the next position.

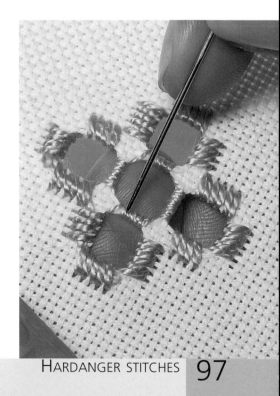

STEP 4 If the wrapping looks uneven, stroke the coils into place with the needle tip. Secure thread ends firmly through the backs of the Kloster blocks, or through the bars themselves.

WOVEN BARS

These are wider and flatter than overcast bars. Choose the finer thread and needle from the table on page 48.

STEP 1 Secure the thread as Step 1 of Overcast Bars (page 97). Bring the needle up at 1, in the middle of the first group of threads to be woven, at the left end of the group.

STEP 2 Make a backstitch over one half of the threads, bringing the needle up again at the center of the threads, to the right of the first stitch.

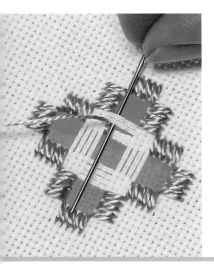

STEP 3 Make a second stitch over the other half of the threads, again bringing the needle up at the center, to the right of previous stitches. Continue weaving over the bar in this way. Count the stitches as you make them and make all the bars the same.

STEP 4 Make the same number of stitches on each half of the bar. Move diagonally on to the next bar, or run the thread through the back of the blocks to reach the next position. Secure thread ends firmly through the backs of bars or Kloster blocks.

WOVEN BARS WITH PICOTS

Picots are little knots formed as a woven bar is stitched, usually one picot at the center of each side.

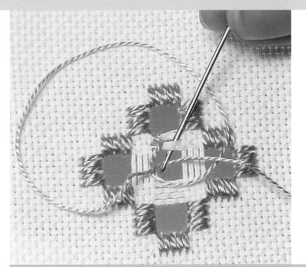

STEP 1 Weave halfway along the bar as for Woven Bars (page 98). Insert the needle for the next stitch and loop the thread around the needle as shown.

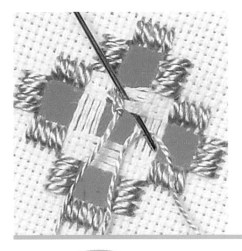

STEP 2 Pull the needle through, forming a little knot on the edge of the bar. Take the needle behind the knot and up through the center of the bar ready for the next stitch.

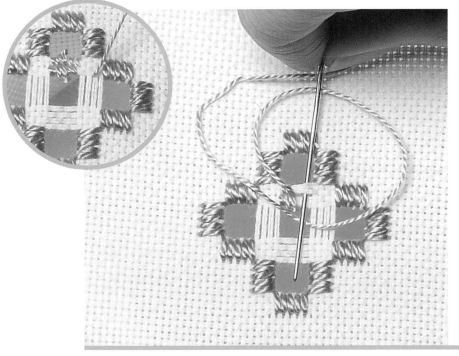

STEP 3 Make another picot in the same way on the next stitch, so that the picot forms on the opposite side of the bar. Count the weaving stitches carefully so that all the picots on all the bars are in the same position. Move diagonally on to the next bar.

LOOP-STITCH FILLING

For this filling four loops are formed, one at the center of each side of an empty square.

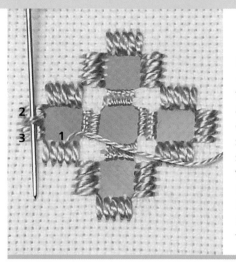

STEP 1 Secure the thread through the back of the Kloster blocks and bring the needle out at the center of a block, up through the empty square at 1. Work clockwise around the square. The first loop shown here is worked onto a Kloster block: pass the needle from top to bottom (2 to 3) under the central stitch of the block, bringing the needle out to the left of the loop of thread.

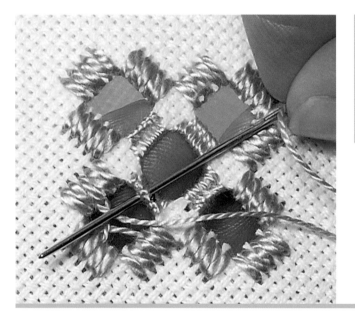

TIP

Some stitchers prefer to work the bars and fillings at the same time, completing the bars around an empty square, then working the filling before moving on to the bars around the next empty square.

STEP 2 On this square, the second side is another Kloster block, so the second loop is worked as above. The third loop is worked into a woven bar: take the needle down through the center of the bar at 4, and bring it up through the empty square, above the loop of thread. If a bar is overcast, simply wrap the needle around it, bringing the needle out above the loop in the same way.

STEP 3 When three loops are complete, pass the needle under the first loop made. Insert the needle to the right of the center stitch of the Kloster block at 5, so that the fourth stitch matches the first. All the loops should twist in the same direction. Pass the needle through the backs of the blocks and/or bars to the next position required.

OBLIQUE LOOP-STITCH FILLING

This filling stitch is worked in a similar way to loop-stitch filling, but the loops are formed at the corners of the empty square.

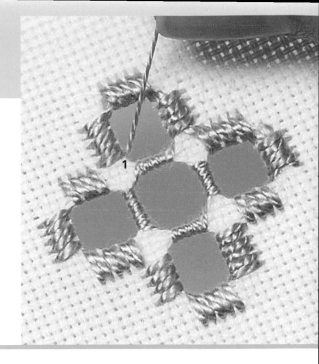

STEP 1 Secure the thread by passing it through the back of three or four Kloster blocks and bring the needle out from beneath the fabric at 1, the corner of an empty square.

STEP 2 Working clockwise around the square, take the needle down at the next corner, one thread intersection in from the corner at 2. Bring the needle up through the loop just formed.

STEP 3 Repeat Step 2 at each of the next two corners. Pass the needle under the first loop made and insert it to match the other corners. All the loops should twist in the same direction. Pass the needle through the backs of the blocks and/or bars to the next position required.

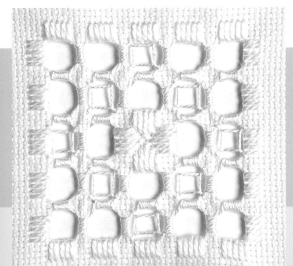

Hardanger work is traditionally stitched in white thread on white fabric, or cream thread on cream fabric. Note the arrangement of Kloster blocks along the straight sides of the square. The bars are overcast, and some of the squares are filled with loop-stitch filling. The central motif is formed by four blocks of satin stitch (see page 110) of varying length, which secure the cut fabric threads in the same way as Kloster blocks.

Dove's-eye filling

This is a very pretty filling, often used in combination with one of the other filling stitches to vary the pattern.

STEP 1 Secure the thread along the back of three or four Kloster blocks and bring the needle up at the corner of an empty square at 1, one thread intersection in from the corner. Insert the needle at the opposite corner (2) and pull quite firmly. Bring the needle out from below the fabric through the empty square, to the left of the diagonal stitch.

STEP 2 Pass the needle several times clockwise around the diagonal thread, overcasting it back to the first corner. Insert the needle back at 1, the first corner.

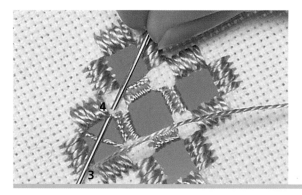

STEP 3 Pass the needle along the back of the block (or bar) to the next empty corner, then bring it up at 3 as before and make a second diagonal stitch across to 4, the opposite corner.

These two heart motifs are worked in random shaded thread. The heart on the left is stitched with woven bars and oblique loop-stitch filling, the other with woven bars and picots, without any filling.

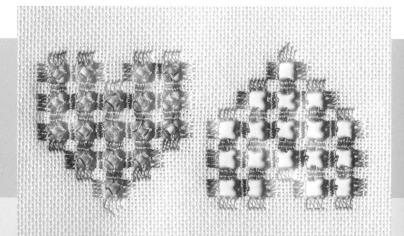

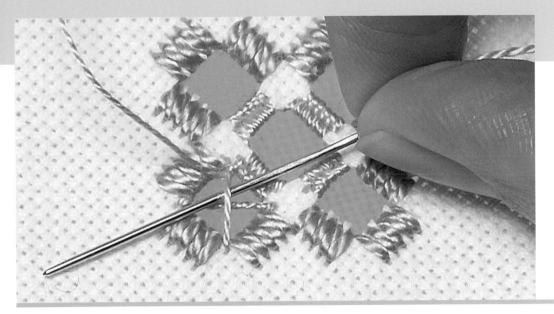

STEP 4 Bring the needle up as before and overcast the second diagonal thread back to the center, not the whole way across.

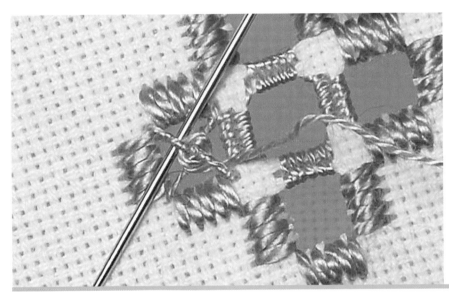

STEP 5 Pass the needle under and over the four "spokes," counterclockwise in a flat spiral, until the spiral almost touches the edges of the empty square, ending at the single thread, the one without overcasting. Count the under and over passes as you make them so that you can make all the dove's eyes the same size.

STEP 6 Overcast the single thread back to the corner and insert the needle to match the other corners. Pass the needle along the backs of the blocks and/or bars to the next position.

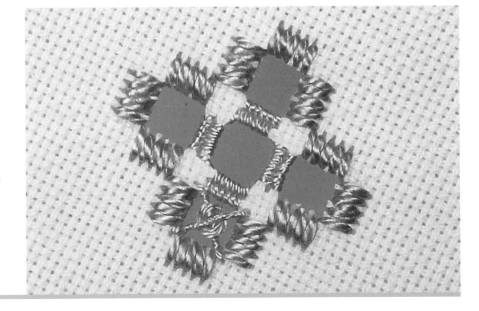

HERRINGBONE STITCH

Use this stitch for a decorative border, or to cover the edge of an appliqué shape. This stitch may be worked on any fabric.

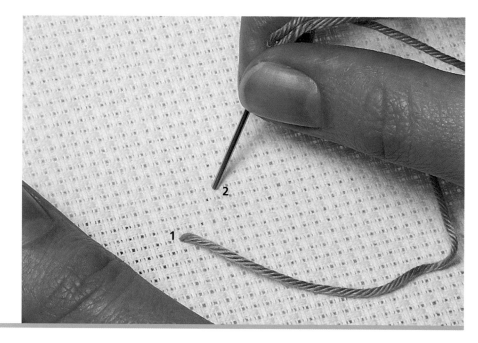

STEP 1
The stitch shown here will form a band four fabric squares deep, although other sizes and proportions are possible. Begin with the waste-knot method (see page 18). Work from left to right. Bring the needle up at lower left at 1 and make a diagonal stitch, across four squares, inserting the needle at 2.

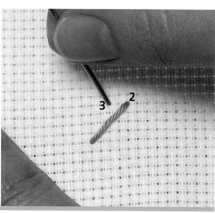

STEP 2
Bring the needle up again at 3, two squares left of 2.

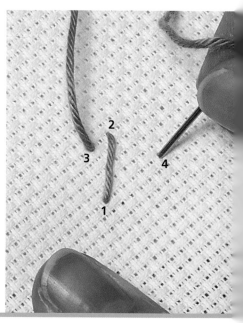

STEP 3
Make a downward diagonal stitch across four squares to 4, six squares right of 1.

Herringbone stitches of various sizes worked on Aida fabric. To turn a square corner as shown, end with a diagonal stitch to the lower line, then bring the needle up above the last insertion, instead of to the left, turn the work, and continue in the new direction. At bottom left, lines of stitches form a pattern of large and small diamonds.

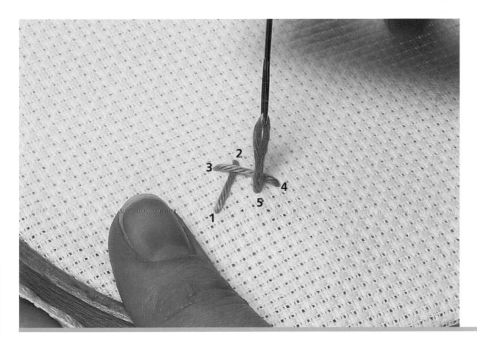

STEP 4
Bring the needle up at 5, two squares left of 4 and four squares below 2.

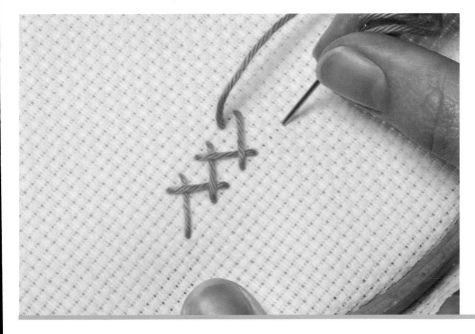

STEP 5
Repeat Steps 1–4. If working on plain fabric, mark two parallel lines of evenly spaced dots to help keep the stitches to a consistent size.

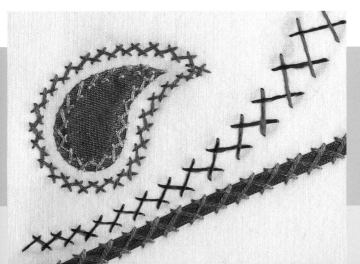

Herringbone stitch is shown here covering the raw edge of the appliqué paisley motif and as an "echo" border. The curved line shows how you can gradually vary the size of the stitches. At bottom right, herringbone stitch holds down a length of ribbon without actually piercing it.

BLANKET STITCH

Use this versatile stitch for decorative borders or to cover the raw edge of an appliqué motif. You can work the stitches close together—often called buttonhole stitch—or space them apart to make spiky lines, or arrange them in circles or squares. You can work this stitch on any fabric.

TIP

On plain fabric mark two parallel lines of evenly spaced dots to keep the size of the stitches constant.

STEP 1
The stitch shown here will form a band four fabric squares deep, with the stitches two squares apart, although you can alter these proportions as you wish. Begin with the waste-knot method (see page 18). Work from left to right. The spikes of the stitches will point away from you. Bring the needle up at 1, the lower left of the required line. Form a loop with the thread as shown and insert the needle at 2, four squares above and two to the right, the end of the first spike.

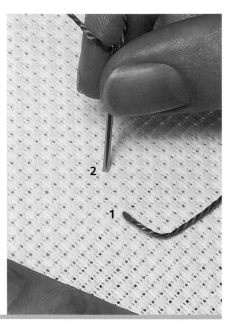

Blanket stitch and variations on Aida fabric. From top to bottom: blanket stitch worked in a straight line; blanket stitch with spikes of varying lengths; blanket stitch arranged in a star, as a closed circle and diamond, and as an overlapping pattern.

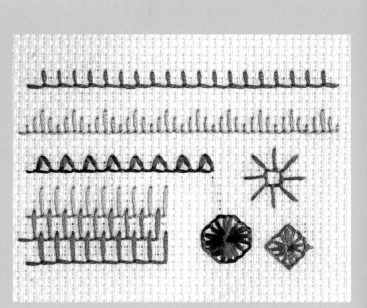

Blanket stitch is used here to cover the raw edge of the appliqué heart, and as an outer "echo" border. Little flower shapes may be circles or ovals, and the baseline of blanket stitch may be whipped, as on the outer border of the heart, or laced, as on two of the flowers, in the same way as for backstitch (see pages 80–81).

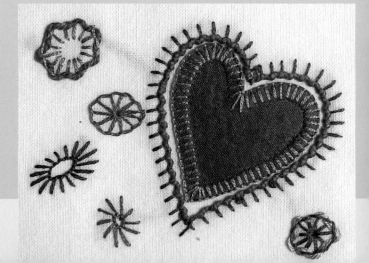

STEP 2 Bring the
needle up again at 3, the
base of the spike, four
squares below 2, inside the
loop of thread.

STEP 3 Pull through
gently. Repeat to the right.

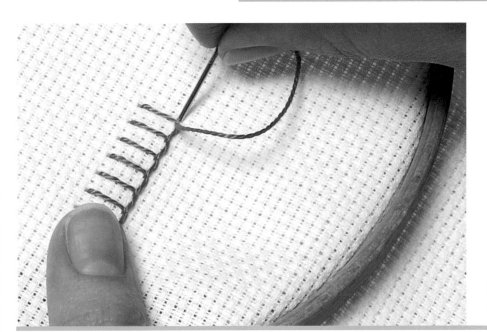

STEP 4 At the end of the
line, hold down the last loop with a
tiny stitch.

Blanket stitch, as the name suggests, makes a good
edging for blankets and other thick, heavy fabrics,
dispensing with the need for a bulky turned hem.
The fabric should be cut straight along a thread to
avoid fraying. Blanket stitch may be worked very
close together—often referred to as buttonhole
stitch—completely covering the fabric beneath,
then the excess fabric can be carefully cut away.

CHAIN AND SINGLE CHAIN STITCHES

Use chain stitch for bold lines, straight or curved. Single chain stitches, sometimes called lazy daisy stitches, may be arranged to form flowers or leaves, or scattered to fill an area. Chain stitch may be worked on any type of fabric.

CHAIN STITCH

STEP 1
Begin with the waste-knot method (see page 18). Work the line of chain stitches from top to bottom, toward you. Bring the needle up at 1, the top of the line. Loop the thread as shown, and insert the needle back in the same place at 1.

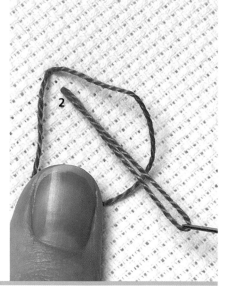

STEP 2
Bring the needle up again at 2, about ⅛ in. (3 mm) below 1—two fabric squares shown here—inside the loop of thread.

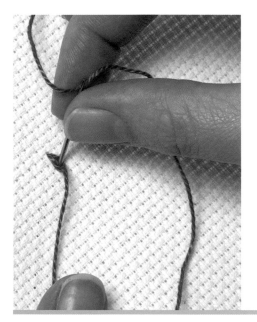

STEP 3
Pull the needle through until the loop lies neatly around the thread. Form another loop and insert the needle again at 2, where it last came out.

On plain fabric, lines of chain stitch may be curved quite tightly. The tighter the curve, the smaller the stitches should be.

OPPOSITE: On Aida fabric, chain stitches may be one, two, or more squares long. They may be worked along straight lines of holes, or stepped to form curves and zigzags.

SAMPLER FILE

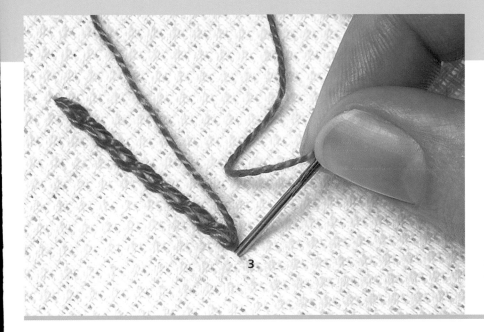

STEP 4
Repeat Steps 2–3 to the end of the line. Hold the last loop in place with a tiny stitch, inserting the needle just outside the last loop at 3.

SINGLE CHAIN STITCH

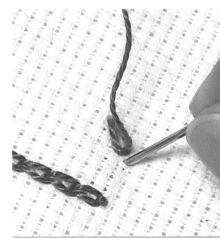

STEP 1
Work just one chain stitch, and hold the loop down with a tiny holding stitch.

STEP 2
For a different effect, make the holding stitch longer, forming a little tail.

TIPS

Chain stitch lines may be marked onto plain fabric as a series of evenly spaced dots, to help keep all the stitches the same size.

On Aida fabric, make the holding stitches half a square long, inserting the needle midway between holes or at the center of a square.

With practice, you can insert the needle and bring it up inside the loop in one movement if your fabric is not too tightly stretched.

SATIN STITCH

Satin stitch is formed with long, straight stitches, worked parallel and close together, often covering the fabric completely. It may be worked on any kind of fabric, but on Aida fabric the choice of thread is crucial if complete coverage of the fabric is required. Stitches on Aida or evenweave fabric may be worked straight with the grain of the fabric, or slanting, usually at 45 degrees.

SATIN STITCH ON AIDA FABRIC OR EVENWEAVE

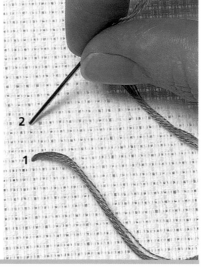

STEP 1
Begin with the waste-knot method (see page 18). Work in a block from left to right. Bring the needle up at the lower edge of the block, at 1, and insert it at the top edge at 2, directly above on the same line of holes. A stitch height of four squares is shown here. Pull through.

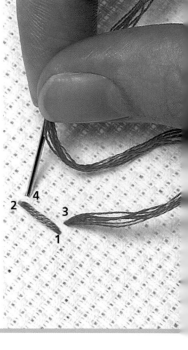

STEP 2
Bring the needle up again on the lower edge at 3, one Aida square or evenweave thread to the right of 1, and insert it on the top edge at 4, one square, or thread, to the right of 2. Pull through.

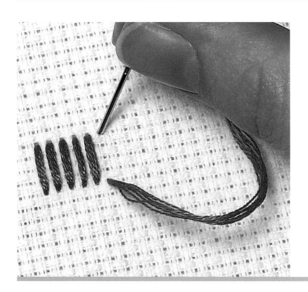

STEP 3
Repeat to the right as required. All the stitches should be parallel.

Satin stitch on evenweave. The top line is worked in random shaded thread. The square blocks of slanting stitches are often called cushion stitch—always work the stitches of each block in the same order. Stitches may be straight with the fabric grain, or slanting, to fill various geometric shapes.

SAMPLER FILE

110   STITCH LIBRARY

SATIN STITCH ON PLAIN FABRIC

STEP 1
On plain fabric it is usual to cover the fabric completely, with no gaps between stitches. Mark the shape to be stitched with a fine outline. Begin with the waste-knot method (see page 18). Begin at the center of the shape: this helps to keep all the stitches slanting at the same angle. Bring the needle up at 1 on the left outside edge of the marked line, and make a slanting stitch across the shape, inserting the needle at 2 on the right outside edge of the marked line. Pull through.

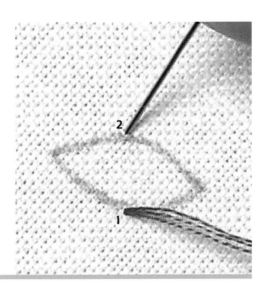

STEP 2
Bring the needle up again on the left edge just above 1 and insert it just above 2. Work a series of stitches in this way up toward the top of the shape. All the stitches should be parallel and close together: lay the thread across the shape as shown, parallel to previous stitches, and insert the needle where the thread crosses the outline.

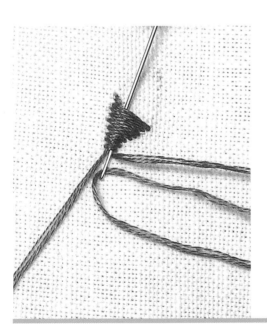

STEP 3
At the top, run the thread through the stitches on the wrong side, back to the center. Then work in the same way down to the bottom of the shape.

On canvas, satin stitches may be straight with the canvas threads, or slanting, normally at 45 degrees. Geometric patterns are simple and quick to work in this stitch.

SHADED SATIN STITCH

This variation is often used to add shading to a leaf or flower petal. The stitches are not quite parallel, but arranged in a fan shape, so they must be very close together to cover the fabric without any gaps.

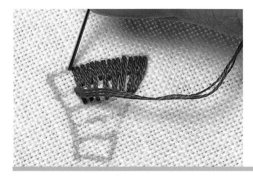

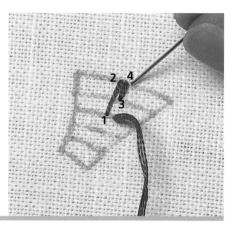

STEP 1
Mark the shape with a fine outline. For three shades of thread, divide the shape with four more lines as shown. Beginning at center top, make a line of long and short satin stitches to the right, bringing the needle up on the second dividing line at 1 for a long stitch, and on the first dividing line at 3 for a short stitch. Always insert the needle on the top line, at 2 and at 4.

STEP 2
Pass the needle through the wrong side of the stitches back to the center, and complete the top line to the left.

STEP 3
Work the second line of stitches in another color, fitting them between the stitches above as shown. These stitches are all the same length, with their lower points positioned alternately on the third and fourth dividing lines. If the shape is sharply tapered, you can skip some stitches, but try to maintain a smooth appearance.

STEP 4
Work the lowest line of stitches in a third color, fitting between those above in the same way. These will be alternate long and short stitches, unless you skip some stitches to fit a tapering shape.

These flower shapes on plain fabric show satin stitch worked to fill the petals, left, and shaded satin stitch, right.

STEM STITCH

As its name suggests, this stitch is ideal for depicting gently curving, sinuous lines such as flower stems. It also makes a good outline stitch for curved shapes. It is normally worked only on plain fabric.

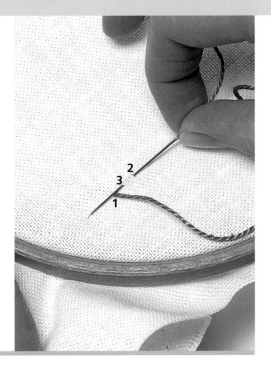

STEP 1
Mark the design on the fabric as a continuous line or a series of evenly spaced dots. Begin with the waste-knot method (see page 18). Work the line from left to right. Bring the needle up at the beginning of the line at 1 and make a small slanting stitch, inserting the needle on the lower edge of the line at 2. Bring the needle out halfway along the previous stitch, on the top edge of the line at 3, above the thread of the previous stitch.

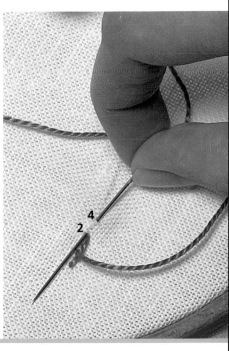

STEP 2
Make another slanting stitch of the same size, slanting across to the lower edge of the line: insert the needle at 4 and bring it out again just above 2.

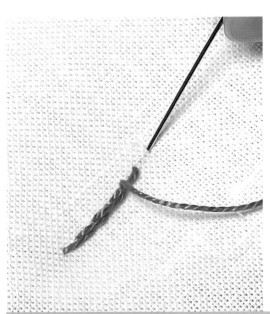

STEP 3
Repeat Step 2 to the end of the line. Each stitch begins above the previous stitch, halfway along its length. If the fabric is not too tightly stretched in a hoop, you can take the needle down and up again in one movement.

TIPS

The tighter the curve, the smaller the stitches need to be. For a wider line you can slant the stitches more sharply, almost like slanting satin stitch (see page 110).

Stem stitch lines in various threads, left to right: perle cotton; three strands of embroidery floss; two strands of embroidery floss; perle cotton No. 5; and one strand of embroidery floss.

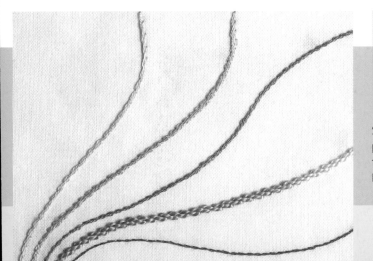

FLY STITCH

This stitch forms a "V" or "Y" shape. It may be worked in lines or scattered at random, or worked closely together to suggest leaf and flower shapes. Fly stitch may be worked on any fabric.

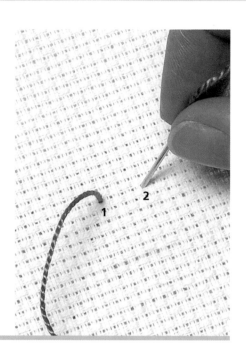

STEP 1
Begin with the waste-knot method (see page 18). Bring the needle up at 1, the top left of the "V," and insert it at 2, top right, forming a loop with the thread as shown.

STEP 2
Bring the needle up at 3, the lower point of the "V," inside the loop of thread.

STEP 3
Pull through to tighten the looped thread, and make a small stitch downward to 4 to hold the loop in place. This small stitch can be kept very short, to make the "V" shape, or lengthened to form a "Y."

SAMPLER FILE

On Aida fabric, fly stitches may be arranged in lines, or to form all-over patterns, or in a circle, like the snowflake pattern shown here.

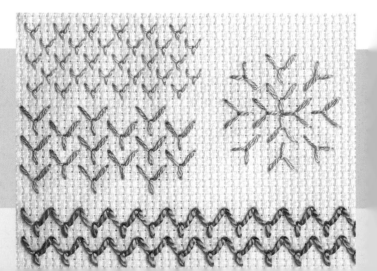

SEEDING STITCH

This simple stitch is used to fill an outline or a background area. It may be evenly scattered, or sprinkled unevenly to add shading. The pairs of stitches are arranged at random, so it is normally used only on plain fabric.

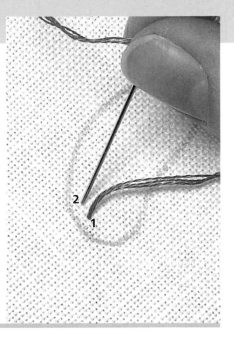

STEP 1 Begin with the waste-knot method (see page 18). Bring the needle up at 1 where required and make a tiny stitch, about ⅛ in. (3 mm) long, inserting the needle at 2.

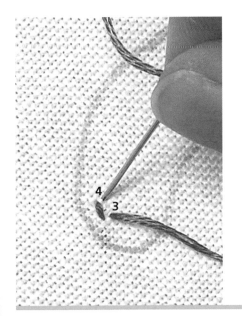

STEP 2 Make another tiny stitch next to the first, from 3 to 4.

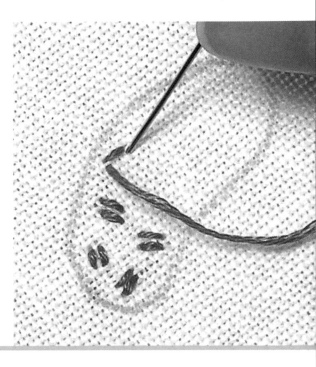

STEP 3 Repeat as required, varying the direction of the stitches at random.

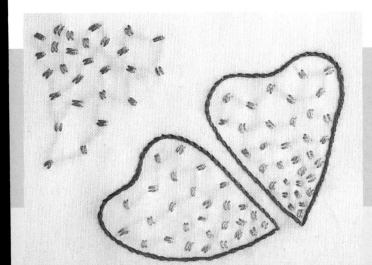

TIP

Work backward and forward to fill an area, avoiding long threads on the back of the work.

The seeding stitches are worked closer together toward the base of the petals, giving a shaded effect. The petal outlines are worked in stem stitch (see page 113).

FRENCH KNOTS

A single French knot makes a bold, raised dot, often used to represent an eye or a flower center. A series of knots may be grouped to form a flower motif, or sprinkled to fill an area with texture. French knots may also be worked with tails. They may be worked on any fabric.

SIMPLE FRENCH KNOT

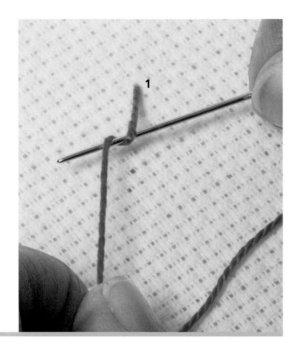

STEP 1 Bring the needle up at 1 and wrap the thread twice around the needle tip. Hold the thread taut with your left hand.

STEP 2 Still holding the thread, insert the needle at 2, very close to 1. Push the needle through to the back of the work, then pull the thread through, keeping the thread taut until you have to let it go. Hold the knot in place with your thumb as you tighten the thread further.

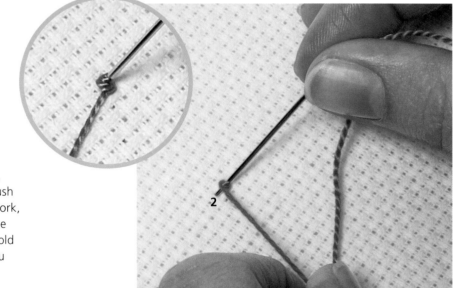

From the left, the first line of knots is worked to cover the holes in the Aida fabric, and the second line to fill the squares. Three flower motifs are worked in French knots, with and without tails, and the right-hand line shows knots with tails three squares long.

FRENCH KNOT WITH TAIL

Work Step 1 of Simple French knot (page 116), but insert the needle at 2, a short distance away from 1. The French knot forms at 2, with its tail stretching back to 1.

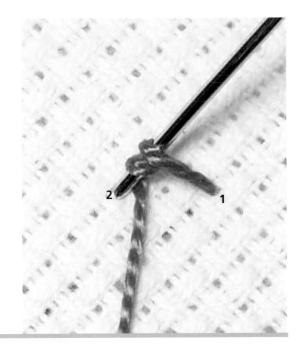

TIPS

On Aida fabric, for a French knot at the center of a square, make point 1 the corner of the square and point 2 the center. For a French knot over a hole, make point 1 halfway between two holes, and point 2 the hole you wish to cover.

On evenweave fabric, always make points 1 and 2 at least one thread apart.

For a larger knot, do not be tempted to wind the thread more than twice because it will be difficult to pull the thread through neatly. Instead, change to a heavier thread, or use more strands.

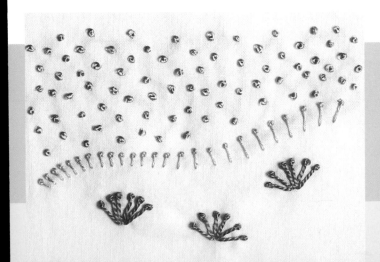

From the top: French knots evenly scattered to fill an area with texture; knots with tails worked in a curved, graded line; and little fans of knots with tails.

BULLION KNOTS

A bullion knot is a short, raised coil. It is also known as caterpillar stitch, worm stitch, coil stitch, and roll stitch. Groups of bullion knots can form flowers or roses, or be arranged in various patterns. These knots may be worked on any type of fabric.

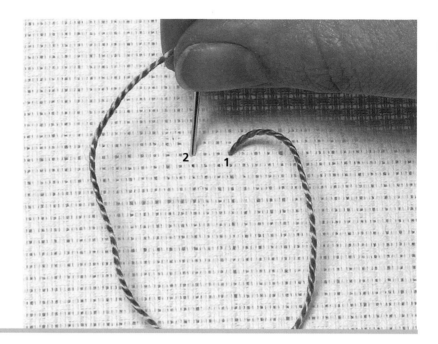

STEP 1
Begin with the waste-knot method (see page 18). Bring the needle through at 1 and insert it at 2, about ¼–⅜ in. (6–10 mm) to the left. Pull it through, leaving a long loop on the surface.

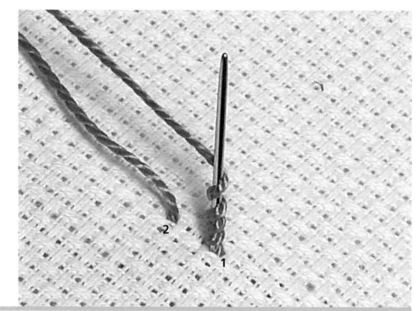

STEP 2
Bring the needle halfway up again at 1 and wind the loop around the tip, about five to eight times. Keep the coils close together, but not overlapping. They should be neat, but not overtight.

Bullion knots, straight or curved, worked on Aida or evenweave fabric, add a bold texture to geometric designs.

OPPOSITE: Bullion roses begin with a triangle of bullion knots at the center. Further knots are added as shown, with two or three extra twists to make them curl.

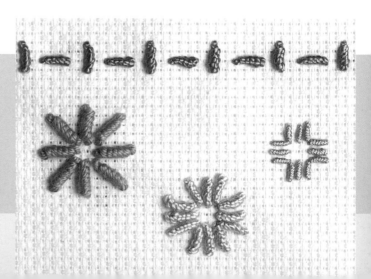

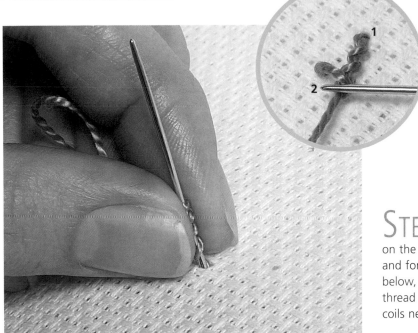

STEP 3
Hold the coils in place on the needle between your left thumb and forefinger. Push the needle up from below, then pull it through. Hold the thread down toward point 2 and pack the coils neatly into place with the needle tip.

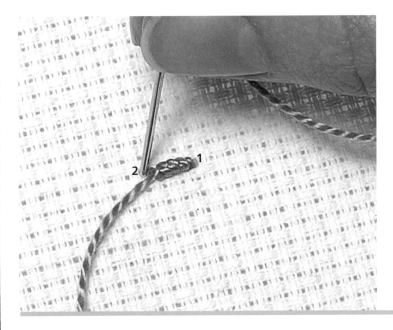

STEP 4
Insert the needle again at 2 and pull it through to the back.

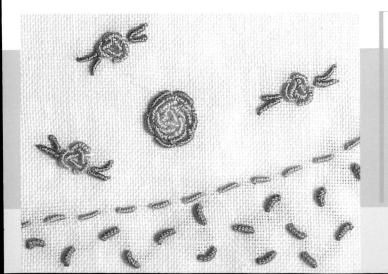

TIPS

The number of coils depends on the distance between 1 and 2 and also on the thickness of thread. More than about eight coils makes the pulling through more difficult, so change to a heavier thread—or more strands—requiring less coils.

To make a curved bullion knot, add two or three extra coils. If you find it difficult to pull the needle through the coils, try a slightly larger needle.

FEATHER STITCH

Feather stitch forms an open, spiky line, used for borders and edgings and also for edging appliqué shapes or covering seams. It may be stitched on any fabric.

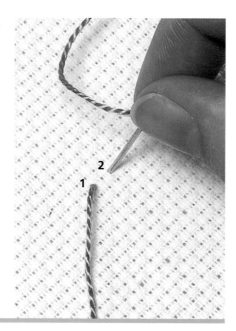

STEP 1
Begin with the waste-knot method (see page 18). Work the line toward you, from top to bottom. Bring the needle up at 1, top center, and insert it at 2, a short distance to the right, on the same level: a distance of two Aida fabric squares is shown here.

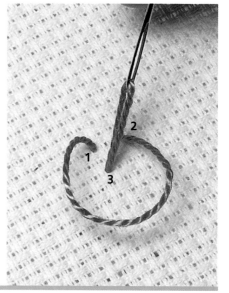

STEP 2
Form a loop with the thread as shown. Bring the needle up on the center line at 3, a short distance below 1, inside the loop of thread. Pull through.

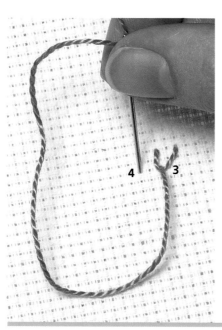

STEP 3
Insert the needle a short distance to the left at 4, on the same level as 3, forming a loop with the thread as shown.

SAMPLER FILE

The four lines on the left show feather stitch worked at various spacings on Aida fabric. The two lines on the right show double feather stitch.

OPPOSITE: Feather stitch is used here on plain fabric to cover the raw edge of an appliqué shape, and also shown worked in a curve.

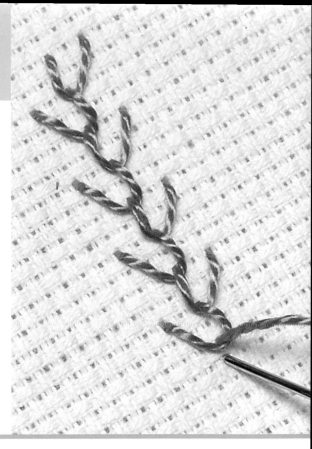

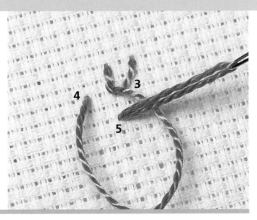

STEP 4
Bring the needle up again at 5 on the center line, a short distance below 3, inside the loop of thread. Pull through.

STEP 5
Repeat these two stitches to the right and left, to the bottom of the line. Hold down the last loop with a small stitch.

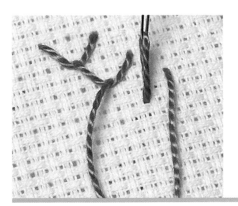

DOUBLE FEATHER STITCH
This variation is worked over five parallel lines.

STEP 1
Beginning at top left, work three feather stitches to the right, always bringing the needle up midway between the ends of the loop and a short distance downward.

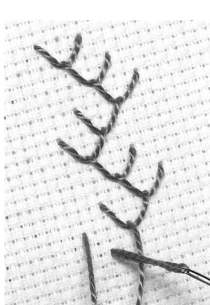

STEP 2
Work two stitches to the left and two to the right alternately down the line.

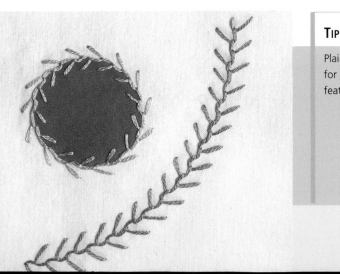

TIP
Plain fabric may be marked with three parallel lines of dots for feather stitch or five parallel lines of dots for double feather stitch, to place the stitches evenly.

Simple couching

Couching, from the French *coucher*, meaning to lay, means stitching a heavy thread to the fabric surface with tiny stitches in another, finer thread. The heavy thread is called the "laid" thread. The finer thread, used to stitch it down, is called the "couching" or "tying" thread. The laid thread may be any thick thread that is difficult to stitch with. For the couching thread, use one or two strands of embroidery floss, or an equivalent fine thread.

Couching may be used to boldly outline an area—especially in blackwork, to cover the edge of an appliqué motif, or simply as a bold line, straight or curved. It is normally worked on plain fabric. Even when worked as a blackwork outline, it is usually stitched with a sharp needle, ignoring the holes of the Aida or evenweave fabric.

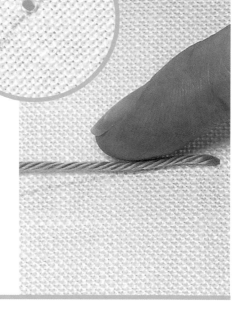

STEP 1
Firmly stretch the fabric in a hoop or frame, preferably held on a stand so that both hands are free. Work a line of couching from right to left, turning the frame as necessary. Use a thick, sharp needle to pierce a hole at the right end of the line at 1, separating the fabric threads without breaking them. Thread the laid (heavy) thread into a suitable needle and bring it up through the hole, leaving a tail of at least 1 in. (2.5 cm) on the wrong side. Lay the thread along the line to the left.

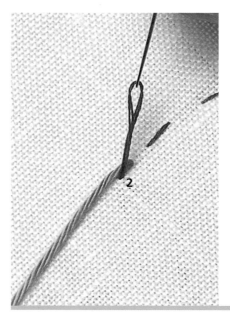

STEP 2
Use a small sharp needle for the couching (thin) thread. Begin with the waste-knot method (see page 18), then baste the tail of laid thread to the wrong side of the fabric, beyond the end of the line, to hold it out of the way. Bring up the needle below the laid thread at 2, a short distance from the beginning of the line.

STEP 3
Make a small vertical couching or tying stitch across the laid thread, inserting the needle at 3, either back down through the same hole as 2 or very close by.

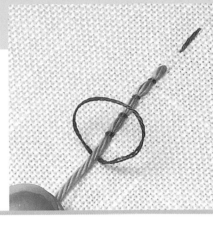

STEP 4
Repeat at equal intervals along the laid thread, holding the laid thread in place with one hand and making the stitches with the other. The couching stitches should not pierce the laid thread.

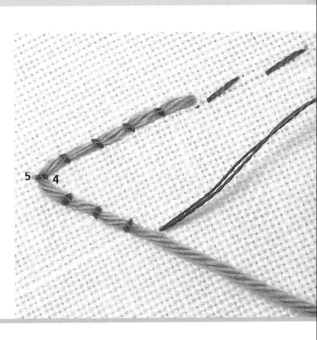

5 4

STEP 5
If you want to turn a sharp corner, position a couching stitch exactly on the corner to hold it in place (from 4 to 5). As you approach a corner, you can adjust the stitch spacing slightly if necessary.

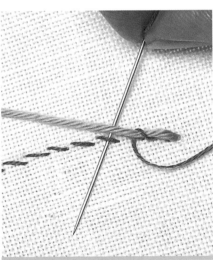

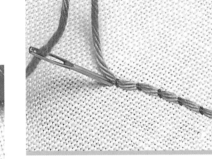

STEP 6
At the end of the line, do not fasten off the couching thread. Pierce another hole as before, thread the laid thread into a suitable needle and take it through to the wrong side.

STEP 7
Trim the laid thread end to about 1 in. (2.5 cm) and fold it back along the line, then use the couching thread to sew it to the backs of the stitches. At the beginning of the line, snip off the waste knot, unpick the basting, and fasten down the beginning of the laid thread in the same way.

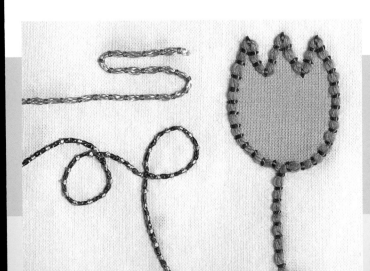

Couched lines may be straight or curved. Here the appliqué tulip has been edged with couching, continued downward to form the flower stem.

GLOSSARY

AIDA FABRIC Evenly woven cotton fabric with regularly spaced holes, forming a grid of squares, used for cross-stitch and other counted thread embroidery.

ANTI-FRAY SOLUTION Special liquid adhesive that dries invisibly, used for extra security of thread ends in difficult situations.

APPLIQUÉ The decoration of fabric by attaching shapes cut from other fabrics.

ASSISI WORK A type of cross-stitch where the background is stitched and the motif left as background fabric.

BASTING Temporary stitching, used to hold fabrics in place until work is complete.

BATTING Natural or synthetic wadding in sheet form, used for quilting.

BIAS BINDING Narrow strips of fabric cut on the bias (i.e. at 45 degrees to the straight grain) and therefore stretchable, pressed with folds for easy use, applied to finish raw fabric edges.

BINCA FABRIC Similar to Aida fabric but with larger squares.

BLACKWORK A type of counted thread embroidery featuring repeating patterns of small straight stitches.

BLENDING FILAMENT Very fine embroidery floss, often glossy or metallic, designed to be combined with other threads.

BLOCKING The damping and stretching of finished work on a padded board (blocking board), to fix its shape.

CANVAS A woven cotton or linen mesh with a regular number of threads (and holes) to the inch in each direction. Normally made from cotton or linen.

CANVASWORK Embroidery worked on evenly woven canvas mesh, with stitches placed regularly by counting canvas threads.

CHENILLE NEEDLE A medium to large needle with a sharp point and a large eye.

COLOR FASTNESS The ability of threads and fabrics to withstand immersion in water without color running.

COTTON The fibers of the cotton plant, used to manufacture sewing threads, embroidery threads, and many fabrics.

COUCHING Attaching a thread or cord to the fabric surface by stitching it down with another thread.

COUNT The number of holes (or threads) to the inch of an evenweave or Aida fabric.

COUNTED THREAD EMBROIDERY Any type of embroidery where stitches are accurately placed on evenweave or Aida fabric by counting the threads or squares.

CREWEL NEEDLE A fine to medium-size needle with a sharp point and an elongated eye.

DUPION A type of silk fabric with a sheen and a slight slub in the weave.

EVENWEAVE FABRIC A fabric woven with the same number of threads to the inch in each direction, used for counted thread embroidery.

FLOSS Embroidery thread supplied as six (or sometimes four) strands, loosely wound together, which may be separated and used individually. Usually cotton or silk.

FREESTYLE EMBROIDERY Any embroidery worked by following design lines, rather than by counting threads.

FUSIBLE WEB A web of non-woven fibers, usually backed with paper, which may be melted with an iron to attach fabric to fabric.

GAUGE The number of holes (or threads) to the inch of a canvas.

HARDANGER FABRIC Similar to Aida fabric, specially treated to ease the withdrawing of threads for Hardanger work.

HARDANGER WORK A type of counted thread openwork embroidery featuring threads cut and drawn in geometric patterns.

HOOP Two wooden rings fitting closely one inside the other, for stretching embroidery fabric while stitching, to prevent puckering.

INTERLINING A non-woven fabric used as a backing, or placed between two layers of fabric, to prevent distortion in use or during stitching.

INTERLOCKING BARS A set of four straight wooden bars that lock together at the corners to form a frame for stretching fabric while working embroidery.

KLOSTER BLOCK A block of 5 satin stitches used in Hardanger work.

LINEN The fibers of the flax plant, used to manufacture fabrics.

PERLE (OR PEARL) COTTON A firmly twisted embroidery thread with a slightly glossy finish, available in several thicknesses.

PERSIAN WOOL Fine embroidery wool usually supplied with three strands wound together in a skein. Strands may be separated and used individually.

PLASTIC CANVAS A plastic mesh resembling woven canvas, but molded in sheets and therefore very stable.

SILK Fibers from the cocoon of the silkworm, used to manufacture embroidery threads and luxury fabrics.

SLATE FRAME A rectangular frame with adjustable rollers on two sides, used for stretching large pieces of work while stitching.

STABILIZER Fabric (normally non-woven) used to back embroidery during stitching, to prevent distortion.

TAPESTRY NEEDLE A medium to large needle with a blunt tip and a large eye.

TAPESTRY WOOL Medium-weight embroidery wool often used for canvaswork.

TUSSAH A type of silk fabric with a slubby, matte finish.

VISCOSE RAYON A man-made fiber derived from cellulose (wood-pulp), used to manufacture glossy embroidery threads and fabrics.

WASTE CANVAS Special canvas that may be pulled apart when wet, used to apply counted thread designs to plain fabric.

WOOL Fibers from the fleece of sheep, used to manufacture woolen threads for embroidery such as Persian wool and Tapestry wool, and also fabrics.

A

Aida fabric 10, 124
  blackwork on 36–37
  counted stitches on
    30–31
  cross-stitch on 26–27
  fan stitch on 110
  needles for 12
  satin stitch on 110
Algerian eye stitch 94
  enlarged 95
anti-fray solution 51, 124
appliqué 74–75, 124
  Chef's apron 76–77
apron 76–77
Assisi work 33
  sachet 34–35

B

backstitch 21, 80
  laced 81
  whipped 81
basting center line 14
Beaded purse 54–55
beads 9, 52, 54
bias binding 23, 124
Binca fabric 10, 124
blackwork 36–37, 124
  Heart napkin 47
  Pot holder 38–39
blanket stitch 39, 106–107
  closed 75
blending threads 9, 53
blocking 20, 124
blocking board 13, 20
Book cover 41
braids 8
bullion knots 118–119
butterfly, Assisi work 33
buttonhole stitch 106, 107

C

canvas 11
  to cut 14
  half cross-stitch on 40
  plastic 11, 125
  ray stitch on 93
  satin stitch on 111
  waste 11, 46

canvaswork 42–43, 124
  needles for 12, 40
  Photo frame 44–45
  threads for 40
chain stitch 108–109
  single 31, 109
Chef's apron 76–77
chenille needles 12, 124
closed blanket stitch 75
cords 8
cotton threads 8
couching, simple 122–123,
  124
counted stitches: on Aida
    fabric 30–31
  on evenweave 32
cross-stitch 86–87
  on Aida fabric 26–27
  on evenweave fabric 32
  Greeting card 28–29
  half 40, 85
  in lines 87
  part 27, 32, 88–89
  Scented sachets 34
  upright 90
  on waste canvas 46
cushion 60–61
cutting 14

D

darning stitch see also
  running stitch
designs: to enlarge or
    reduce 58
  to trace 58
  to transfer 62–63
diamond ray stitch 93
double feather stitch 121
double running stitch 33,
    36, 82–83
dove's eye filling 102–103

E

echo border 105, 106
enlarged Algerian eye stitch
    94
equipment 12–13
evenweave fabric 10, 32,
    36, 124

cross-stitch on 32
  needles for 12
  satin stitch on 110
  Scented sachets 34–35
eyelet pattern 31

F

fabric glue 45
fabrics 10–11
  to cut 14
  see also Aida; canvas;
    evenweave
fan stitch 92
feather stitch 120–121
  double 121
finishing techniques 21–23
fish picture, blackwork
    36–37
floss 8, 9, 124
  to handle 17
Flowery T-shirt 72–73
fly stitch 114
Framed portrait 66–67
frames: interlocking bar 13,
    42, 124
  to mount fabric in 16
  slate 13, 125
fraying, to prevent 14, 51
French knots 31, 116
  with tail 117
fusible web 74, 124

G

gauge, canvas 11, 124
Greeting card 28–29

H

half cross-stitch 40, 85
  Book cover 41
hanging loop 35, 39
Hardanger fabric 10, 124
Hardanger stitches 96–103
Hardanger work 48–49, 124
  Trinket box 50–51
heart motif 46
Heart napkin 47
hemstitch 23
herringbone stitch 104–105
hoops 13, 59, 124

frame 15
  to mount fabric in 15
  stitching method 19

I

interfacing 68
interlocking bar frame 13,
    42, 124
iron-on interfacing 68
iron-on transfers 62

K

Kloster blocks 48–49, 96,
    124

L

lazy daisy stitch see also
  single chain stitch
lightbox 58
loop stitch filling 100
  oblique 51, 101

M

markers 13
metallic threads 9, 53
motifs 40, 46, 74–75

N

napkin 46–47
needles 12, 13
  for Aida fabric 12
  for canvas 40
  for cross-stitch 26
  for freestyle embroidery
    12, 59
  for Hardanger work 48
  to thread 17, 53

O

oblique loop stitch filling
    51, 101
overcast bars 49, 51, 97

P

part cross-stitch 27, 88–89
  on evenweave 32
perle cotton 8, 124
  to handle 17
Persian wool 9, 42, 125

Photo frame 44–45
photocopying 58
photo-transfers 64–65
pins 12
plain weave fabrics 11
    to embroider using waste
        canvas 46, 47
    satin stitch on 111
plastic canvas 11, 125
Pot holder 38–39
pressing 20
printed fabrics, motifs from
    75
purse 54–55

Q
quarter cross-stitch 89

R
Rabbit cushion 60–61
ray stitch 93
ready-mades, to embroider
    71
right side out, to turn 22
ruler 13
running stitch 84
    double 33, 36, 82–83

S
satin stitch: on Aida fabric
    110
    on plain fabric 111
    shaded 112
Scented sachets 34–35
scissors 12, 14
seams 21
seeding stitch 115
self-adhesive stabilizer 69
sequins 9, 52, 54
sewing machine 13
silky threads 9
single chain stitch 31, 109
slate frame 13, 125
slip stitch 21
slip-through-the-back
    method 18
Sparkly beaded purse 54–55
sprigs 83
stabilizers 68, 71, 125

self-adhesive 69
    water-soluble 70
star stitch 91
stem stitch 113
stitch-to-the-knot method 18
stitches: Algerian eye 94–95
    back 21, 80–81
    blanket 39, 106–107
    bullion knots 118–119
    chain 108–109
    cross 86–87, 90
    double feather 121
    double running 33, 36,
        82–83
    fan 92
    feather 120–121
    fly 114
    French knots 31, 116–117
    half cross 40, 85
    Hardanger 96–103
    hem 23
    herringbone 104–105
    part cross 27, 32, 88–89
    ray 93
    running 84
    satin 110–112
    seeding 115
    single chain 31, 109
    slip 21
    star 91
    stem 113
stitching methods 19
strawberry motif 40, 41

T
T-shirt 72–73
tape measure 13
tapestry needles 12, 125
tapestry wool 9, 125
thimble 13
thread(s) 8–9, 13
    for canvas 40
    coverage 42
    for cross-stitch 26
    to fasten off 18
    for freestyle embroidery 59
    to handle 17
    for Hardanger work 48
    to lock onto needle 53

special 53
    to start 18
    to untwist 43
three-quarter cross-stitch 32,
    88–89
tracing 58
transfers 62–63
Trinket box 50–51
troubleshooting 20
turning right side out 22
tweezers 12

U
unpicking 20
upright cross-stitch 90

W
waste canvas 11, 125
    cross-stitch on 46
waste-knot method 18
water-soluble pen 58, 59
water-soluble stabilizers 70
whipping 37, 81
window card mount 28–29,
    66, 67
wools 9
woven bars 98
    with picots 99

RESOURCES

With thanks to the following companies who supplied materials for this book:

Coats Crafts UK
DMC Creative World Ltd.
Rowan: The Kaffe Fassett Fabric Collection
Lazertran UK
Dylon International

Here's a handy list of web sites where you can find helpful embroidery information and supplies:

Coats and Clark (for threads, yarns, fabrics, canvas, stabilizers)
www.coatsandclark.com

The DMC Corporation (for threads, yarns, fabrics, canvas)
www.dmc.com

Dylon International (for photo-transfer paste and paper)
www.dylon.com

Kreinik Manufacturing Co. Inc. (for metallic and silk threads)
www.kreinik.com

Lazertran LLC (USA) (for photo-transfer papers)
www.lazertran.com

Madeira USA Ltd. (for threads, accessories)
www.madeirausa.com

Rowan: The Kaffe Fassett Fabric Collection (for plain and patterned cotton fabrics)
www.knitrowan.com

Sulky (for stabilizers)
www.sulky.com

Tristan Brooks Designs (for silk threads, accessories)
www.TristanBrooks.com

For craft stores in the United States, listed by zip code, try www.i-craft.com